The Man Who Stopped Time

BOOK 2 OF THE
ADULT LEARNER SERIES

The Man Who Stopped Time

JUDITH ANDREWS GREEN
SUPERVISOR,
READING CLINIC
UNIVERSITY OF MAINE,
FARMINGTON

JAMESTOWN PUBLISHERS
PROVIDENCE, RHODE ISLAND

Catalog No. 201

The Man Who Stopped Time

Copyright © 1979 by
Judith Andrews Green

Cover Design by Stephen R. Anthony
Cover Illustration and
Story Illustrations by David Ireland

Printed in the United States
on Recycled Paper

79 80 81 82 9 8 7 6 5 4 3 2 1

ISBN 0-89061-173-4

Titles in This Series

To Jake
who comes from a very special family
and
to Dick and Paul
who knew Sam from the beginning

TO THE READER

Sam found out he could stop time. These stories are about Sam. The stories tell what happened to Sam when he stopped time.

You will meet Sam's girlfriend, June, a policeman named Webb, and . . . the man with the scar.

Before each story begins, there are words for you to look at and learn. These words are in sentences so you can see how they will be used in the story. After each story there are questions for you to answer. These questions will give you an idea of how well you are reading.

Another part that comes with each story is called Language Skills. These parts are lessons which will help you to read, write and spell better.

The last two parts with every story deal with Life Skills. These are things you need to know about and know how to do to get along in life.

The answers to all the questions and exercises are in the back of the book. This lets you check your answers to see if they are right.

We hope you will like reading *The Man Who Stopped Time* and learning all of the things this book teaches.

CONTENTS

Story 6

How to Use This Book

1. Learn the Preview Words

Say the words in the box. Then read the sentences. Try to learn the words. See if you know what each sentence means.

2. Read the Story

As you read, try to follow the story and what the people in it are doing. See how being able to stop time changes Sam's life.

3. Answer: Comprehension Questions

Put an *x* in the box next to the best answer to each question. Read all ten questions first and answer the easy ones. Then go back and answer the hard ones.

4. Correct Your Answers

Use the Answer Key on page 169. If your answer is wrong, circle that box and put an *x* in the right box.

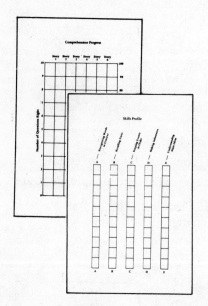

5. Fill in the Graphs

Fill in the graph on page 187 to show your comprehension score. Use the graph on page 189 to chart your skills.

6. Read: Language Skills

This comes after the questions. Read the pages and do the exercises. Use the Answer Key on page 171 to correct the exercises.

7. Read: Understanding Life Skills

Read these pages and follow the step-by-step lessons. Use the Answer Key on page 175 to check your answers.

(Sample page shown)

1. Understanding Life Skills

Savings Accounts

If you have some money, the best place to put it is in the bank. It will be safe. Even if the bank is robbed, you can get your money back. And while your money is in the bank, it will make more money. The bank will pay you *interest.* For example, let's say you put $100 in a bank that pays 5% interest. At the end of a year, the interest will be $5. The bank will pay you $5 in interest. Then you will have $105.

Some banks pay more than others. Before you pick a bank to put your money in, you should find out which bank has the highest interest rate. You can call some of the banks near you and ask what rate of interest they pay on savings accounts. Then you can pick the bank with the highest percent.

To open a regular savings account, first pick the bank you want. Take your money to the counter. Tell the person behind the counter that you want to start a savings account. The teller will give you a card to fill out that looks like the one on the next page.

Signature. The first line says, "Sign here." This means write your name. You must write, not print. Who signed the card in the example?

Social Security Number. On the same line which asks you to sign your name are the letters S.S. No. This stands for "social security number." Copy this carefully from your social security card. What is June's social security number?

8. Practice: Applying Life Skills

Read the instructions and do the Life Skills exercise. Take your time. Do the work carefully. Try to remember what you just read about understanding life skills. Use the Answer Key on page 179 to correct the exercise.

1. Applying Life Skills

Opening a Savings Account

When you open a savings account at a bank, you will be asked to fill out a card like this. As you do the steps below, make sure all the facts are clear. When you are done, change cards with someone in your class to see if everything is right and easy to read.

FRANKLIN SAVINGS BANK

S.S. No. ____

Sign here ____

Address ____

Birthplace ____   Mother's Maiden Name ____   Date of Birth ____

Father's Name ____

Name of Husband or Wife ____   Occupation ____

Date ____

Step 1 Sign here. Write your first name, the first letter of your middle name and your last name. Be careful to write; do not print.

Step 2 S.S. No. Write your social security number.

9. Read the Story Again

Go back to the story and read it once more. This time, as you read, try to feel all the interest and excitement the writer has built in.

Then, go on to the Preview Words for the next story.

1. The Man Who Stopped Time

The first time he stopped time, Sam did not even know what had happened.

He was walking down the street. It was a nice day, but Sam was not happy. He was angry at his girlfriend, and that made him angry at everyone. He was walking and looking down at the ground. "I wish it would all stop," he thought. "I wish everyone would just stop and let me be alone."

A funny feeling came over Sam. He looked up. Everyone *had* stopped!

A man was standing right in front of Sam. He looked as if he were walking. One foot was up in the air. But he was not walking. He was standing still, looking in front of him.

Sam turned around. Everyone on the street had stopped. They all looked as if they were walking, but they were standing still. Some of them looked as if they were talking, but Sam could not hear a thing.

Everything had stopped.

Sam walked down the street. He walked around everyone on the street. They all looked as if they had been turned to stone. No one said anything.

Sam even saw a bird. It was hanging in the air as if it had a string to hold it up.

Then Sam saw a dog. It looked as if it were running, but it was standing still. Sam went up to it. He stood and looked at it for a long time. Then he patted it. It looked as if it were made of stone, but it was warm.

"Maybe I am asleep," Sam thought. "Maybe I will wake up, and I will be in my bed." But he knew that he was not asleep.

1. Preview Words

Study the words in the box. Then read the sentences below with your teacher. Look carefully at the words with lines under them.

course	jewelry	only	talking
everything	know	people	thought
forever	money	ready	watch
front	move	said	where
hanging	once	stupid	would

1. Sam did not even <u>know</u> what had happened.
2. I wish it <u>would</u> all stop.
3. They looked as if they were <u>talking</u>.
4. <u>Everything</u> has stopped.
5. No one <u>said</u> anything.
6. A bird was <u>hanging</u> in the air.
7. "Maybe I am asleep," Sam <u>thought</u>.
8. Why am I the <u>only</u> one who can move?
9. <u>People</u> were walking and talking and cars were going by.
10. When you stop time, people are <u>stupid</u>.
11. Now Sam was <u>ready</u> to steal something big.
12. He went to a <u>jewelry</u> store.
13. Sam, <u>where</u> did you get this ring?
14. "Of <u>course</u> not!" he said.
15. I will steal lots of <u>money</u>.
16. You should <u>watch</u> where you are going.
17. He found himself in <u>front</u> of June's house.
18. She did not <u>move</u>.
19. I <u>would</u> be all alone <u>forever</u>.
20. Everyone was talking at <u>once</u>.

1. The Man Who Stopped Time

The first time he stopped time, Sam did not even know what had happened.

He was walking down the street. It was a nice day, but Sam was not happy. He was angry at his girlfriend, and that made him angry at everyone. He was walking and looking down at the ground. "I wish it would all stop," he thought. "I wish everyone would just stop and let me be alone."

A funny feeling came over Sam. He looked up. Everyone *had* stopped!

A man was standing right in front of Sam. He looked as if he were walking. One foot was up in the air. But he was not walking. He was standing still, looking in front of him.

Sam turned around. Everyone on the street had stopped. They all looked as if they were walking, but they were standing still. Some of them looked as if they were talking, but Sam could not hear a thing.

Everything had stopped.

Sam walked down the street. He walked around everyone on the street. They all looked as if they had been turned to stone. No one said anything.

Sam even saw a bird. It was hanging in the air as if it had a string to hold it up.

Then Sam saw a dog. It looked as if it were running, but it was standing still. Sam went up to it. He stood and looked at it for a long time. Then he patted it. It looked as if it were made of stone, but it was warm.

"Maybe I am asleep," Sam thought. "Maybe I will wake up, and I will be in my bed." But he knew that he was not asleep.

It was very quiet. There was no sound anywhere. Sam knew that everything had stopped all over the city. He did not know what to do. He was very lonely.

Sam sat down on the front step of a house. He put his head in his hands so that he would not have to look at all the stone people. He wanted to cry.

"Why did this happen?" he said to himself. "What made it happen? Why am I the only one who can move?"

Sam sat for a long time with his head in his hands. At last he said, "I wish that I had not had a fight with June. Will I ever see her again? Will I ever see anyone again? Or will I have to live all alone forever? Oh, how I wish that everything would start again. I will die like this."

Suddenly Sam could hear a sound—lots of sounds. He could hear the hum of cars, people talking, the sound of feet on the street. He looked up. Everything was going again. People were walking and talking, and cars were going by. Everyone looked as if nothing had happened. One man saw Sam sitting on the step and gave him a very funny look, but that was all. Sam was so happy that he ran all the way to June's house.

At first Sam was too happy to think about what had happened. That night he sat down to think about it. What made everything stop? What made it happen?

Sam could not sleep. All he could think about was how everything looked when everything stopped.

He thought about it all night. It was getting light when he went to sleep. When he woke up, he went right on thinking about it.

Suddenly he thought, "I wished it! I wished that everything would stop, and it did. Then I wished that it would start again, and it started. I wished it!"

He jumped up. He could not wait. He ran out into the street. Everything was moving.

"I wish that everything would stop," he said.

Everything did.

People were stopped. Cars were stopped. There was no sound anywhere.

"I wish that everything would start again," Sam said.

Everything did.

Sam spent the rest of the day stopping everything and starting it again. He wanted to find out everything he could do.

He threw a stone up in the air. Then he wished that everything would stop, and the stone stayed up. When he wished that everything would start again, it fell down.

He found out that he could scare people. He wished everything would stop. Then he walked down the street and stopped right in front of a man. Then he started everything again. The man looked scared. He thought that Sam had suddenly popped out of the air.

Sam made everything stop, and then he looked at a clock. It was not running. When he made everything start, the clock started running again.

"I can stop time!" Sam thought. "I can make time stop, and I can still move. I can step outside time!"

He thought about it for a long time. At last he thought, "I can do anything I want to, and no one can stop me."

The next day Sam thought he would try something new. He went to a store and looked around. "I would like a new pen," he thought.

He went to a part of the store where no one could see him. He did not want anyone to see him pop out of the air. Then he stopped time. He walked by all the stone people to the rack where the pens were.

"All the people look so funny," Sam thought. "They are standing there looking at nothing. They look funny with their mouths open. When you stop time, people are stupid."

Sam took a pen out of the rack and went back to the same part of the store. He started time again. No one knew that he had the pen.

Sam walked down the street, holding the pen in his hand. "I can take anything I want," he thought. "No one can stop me."

He walked down the street, looking at the stores. "Before I take anything more, I should try something," he thought.

He stood still. He thought about the way he was standing. He thought about where his arms were, and where his legs were. Then he waited until a man was looking right at him. He stopped time and then walked around the man. He went back to the same spot where he had been standing.

He was careful to put his arms and legs back the same way they were before. Then he started time again. The man who was looking at him did not know that he had moved.

Now Sam was ready to steal something big. He went to a jewelry store. He went to the counter and looked at all the rings. "I will take this one," he thought. "June will like this one."

Sam thought about the way he was standing, and then he stopped time. He went in back of the counter and took the ring.

He was about to start time again when he looked at the man who ran the store. The man was standing by the counter with his mouth open. He had been talking to someone, but now he was stopped, quiet. "He looks like someone on TV with the sound turned off," Sam thought. He went up to the man and made a face at him.

"That was fun," Sam said to himself as he went back to the place where he had started. Then he started time again and walked out of the store as if he did not want anything.

"June will like this ring," he thought. "Wait until she sees it." He went to her house and rang the doorbell.

"Sam!" June said when she opened the door. "Where have you been for the last two days?"

"I have had a lot to do," Sam said. "But I have something for you." He showed her the ring.

"Oh! How pretty!" June said. "Thank you so much—it makes me so happy."

"Put it on and see how it looks," said Sam.

June tried to put it on. "Oh, Sam, it is too small," she said.

"See, it will not go on. Maybe you can take it back to the store and get a bigger one."

"No!" said Sam.

"Why not?"

"I—I—well . . ." Sam could not think of anything to say.

"Sam, where did you get this ring? It must have cost a lot. Sam, did you—did you steal it?"

"Of course not!" he said, looking down at his feet.

"Sam, look at me. Did you steal it?" He did not say anything. "Oh, Sam, how could you?" June started to cry.

"Come on, June," Sam said. "I just . . ."

"Go away! Go away and take the ring with you!" June pushed Sam out and slammed the door.

Sam walked down the street feeling very sad. Then he started to get angry. "I will show her," he thought. "I will steal lots of money. I will be very rich. I will have everything I want. That will show her."

Sam knew that robbing a bank would be very easy for him now. "I can just walk in and take the money," he said to himself. "No one will know that I am there. I will be the best bank robber there ever was."

He was walking and thinking about how much money he would steal. Suddenly, someone bumped into him. "You should watch where you are going," the man said.

That made Sam feel even more angry. He walked very fast. He wished that everyone would go away. "I will make them stop," he said. "Everything stop!" Everything did.

That was better. He walked around the stone people and made faces at them. He walked around for a long time.

It was very quiet. Very, very quiet.

He walked some more. Nothing moved.

He found himself in front of June's house. He went in. He looked for June. She was sitting in a chair, looking down at her hands. Her eyes were red—she had been crying for a long time.

She did not move.

It was very, very quiet.

"June," Sam said.

She could not hear him.

She did not move.

Sam ran out of the house. He ran down the street, ran and ran. Suddenly he felt a bump, a very small one. He looked down. A little bird was lying at his feet. "I must have bumped it right out of the air," he thought.

He took a step back. "I wish that time would start again," he said. He could hear people walking and talking. He could hear cars going by. Everything was moving again. But the little bird did not move.

Sam picked it up. It was dead.

Sam could not help it—he began to cry. He sat down on the front steps of a house, holding the bird in his hand and crying.

Then he sat still for a long time, thinking. "What if I bumped into a person? Would the person be dead?

"What if I could not start time again? Would I have to live like that forever? I would never hear anyone talk, ever again. No one would move. I would be all alone forever."

Now he was afraid. "I will not stop time again."

Suddenly he could hear the sound of a car, and someone screamed. A little girl had run out in the street, and a car was about to hit her. "Time, stop!" Sam said. He ran out in the street. The girl was there, as still as stone. Her eyes were very big. Her face showed how scared she was.

"Can I move her?" thought Sam. "Will she be dead when time starts again?" He did not know what to do, and no one could tell him. There was the car, just about to hit her. "If the car hits her, she will die anyway," Sam thought. He picked her up, very slowly and carefully. He moved her just a little bit, so that the car would miss her. He put her down very carefully, just the way she had been before. Then he went back to where he had been sitting. He put his head in his hands. He did not want to look. Then he started time again.

The little girl was running again. The car did not hit her, but went on down the street. The little girl's mother ran out and put her arms around the girl. She was crying. Everyone was talking at once. The mother said over and over, "I thought it was going to hit her! Oh, I was so afraid that it was going to hit her!"

Sam walked away, feeling very good. "There is one more thing I have to do," he thought. He went back to the jewelry store. He stopped time, put the ring back, and started to go out again. Then he looked at the man in back of the counter. "I am sorry," he said. Then he went out and started time again.

At last he could go to June's house again. When he rang the doorbell, he was afraid of what she would say. But when she opened the door, she was happy to see him.

"I gave the ring back," he told her. "I will never do anything like that again." June did not say anything. She just gave him a big hug.

"And I will not stop time again—unless I have to!" Sam thought. He was very happy.

1. Comprehension Questions

Directions. Answer these questions about the story you have just read. Put an *x* in the box beside the best answer to each question.

1. Sam did not want to look at all the <u>stone</u> <u>people</u>. Stone
(A) people are
   - ☐ a. made of stone.
   - ☐ b. not moving.
   - ☐ c. not alive.
   - ☐ d. frozen.

2. Sam sat for a long time with his <u>head</u> <u>in</u> <u>his</u> <u>hands</u>. How
(A) did Sam feel?
   - ☐ a. Sad
   - ☐ b. Sleepy
   - ☐ c. Bored
   - ☐ d. Angry

3. When did Sam find out what made time stop?
(C)
   - ☐ a. The same day
   - ☐ b. That night before he fell asleep
   - ☐ c. The next day when he woke up
   - ☐ d. Two days after it happened

4. Sam found out that when he stopped time he
(E)
   - ☐ a. had nothing to do.
   - ☐ b. could step into the past.
   - ☐ c. had power over everyone.
   - ☐ d. could make people do what he liked.

5. What did June say to Sam when she found out he stole
(B) the ring?

    ☐ a. Oh! How pretty! Thank you so much.

    ☐ b. It is too small. Can you get a bigger one?

    ☐ c. I don't like it. Take the ring back!

    ☐ d. Go away and take the ring with you!

6. Which of these things did Sam do last?
(C) ☐ a. Bump into a bird

    ☐ b. Steal a ring

    ☐ c. Rob a pen

    ☐ d. Give June a gift

7. Sam says, "I will not stop time again." Soon after, he
(B) does stop time again. Why?

    ☐ a. He wanted to rob a bank.

    ☐ b. He was angry at everyone.

    ☐ c. June asked him to stop time.

    ☐ d. A car was about to hit a little girl.

8. As the story ends, June
(D) ☐ a. is sorry.

    ☐ b. forgives Sam.

    ☐ c. does not like Sam.

    ☐ d. thinks stealing is all right.

9. By the end of the story, Sam feels it is wrong to stop
(E) time

    ☐ a. even to help someone.

    ☐ b. just to take the ring back.

    ☐ c. even to stop a crime.

    ☐ d. only to do something bad.

10. What kind of person do you think Sam really is? He is
(D) someone who
    ☐ a. thinks only of himself.
    ☐ b. wants to do the right thing.
    ☐ c. can not think for himself.
    ☐ d. likes money best of all.

Skills Used to Answer Questions

A. Recognizing Words in Context   B. Recalling Facts

C. Keeping Events in Order   D. Making Inferences

E. Understanding Main Ideas

1. Language Skills

Singular Possessives

Look at this sentence from the story you have just read:

At last he could go to June's house again.

Whose house did Sam go to? He went to the house which belongs to June. The 's shows that June owns the house.

When we want to show that someone owns something, we add 's. The mark (') is called an apostrophe.

Exercise 1

Show ownership by adding 's. The first one has been done.

1. the car which belongs to the man

   the _____*man's*_____ _____*car*_____

2. the house which belongs to Sam

   _____ _____

3. the bike which belongs to the boy

   the _____ _____

4. the coat which belongs to June

   _____ _____

5. the gun which belongs to Webb

   _____ _____

6. the store which belongs to Jackson

   _____ _____

Now look at this sentence:

The little <u>girl</u>'s <u>mother</u> ran after her.

In this sentence, *the girl's mother* is a shorter way of saying *the mother of the girl.* Use 's to mean *of the.*

Exercise 2

Use 's to make these phrases shorter and easier to read. The first one has been done for you.

1. the <u>girlfriend</u> of <u>Sam</u>

   Sam's   *girlfriend*

2. the <u>eyes</u> of the <u>girl</u>

   the _____ _____

3. the <u>smile</u> of the <u>man</u>

   the _____ _____

4. the <u>father</u> of the <u>boy</u>

   the _____ _____

5. the <u>size</u> of the <u>ring</u>

   the _____ _____

6. the <u>wings</u> of the <u>bird</u>

   the _____ _____

7. the <u>fur</u> of the <u>dog</u>

   the _____ _____

8. the <u>horn</u> of the <u>car</u>

   the _____ _____

Exercise 3

Look at the words with lines under them. As you copy these sentences, use 's to say the same thing in a shorter way. Then put a line under the word with 's. Look at the examples in the box before you begin.

The <u>hands</u> <u>of</u> <u>the</u> <u>clock</u> stopped.

The <u>clock's</u> hands stopped.

The <u>gun</u> <u>which</u> <u>belongs</u> to the man fell.

The <u>man's</u> gun fell.

---

1. <u>Money</u> <u>which</u> <u>belongs</u> <u>to</u> <u>the</u> <u>bank</u> was in a bag.

2. The <u>motor</u> <u>of</u> <u>the</u> <u>car</u> had stopped.

3. Sam was taken to the <u>hide-out</u> <u>which</u> <u>belongs</u> <u>to</u> <u>the</u> <u>gang</u>.

4. The <u>smile</u> <u>of</u> <u>the</u> <u>man</u> was mean.

5. He could hear the <u>motor</u> <u>of</u> <u>the</u> <u>boat</u>.

6. Sam went to <u>the</u> <u>house</u> <u>which</u> <u>belongs</u> <u>to</u> <u>his</u> <u>girlfriend</u>.

7. The <u>mother</u> <u>of</u> <u>Timmy</u> was scared.

8. The <u>father</u> <u>of</u> <u>the</u> <u>boy</u> got a call.

9. The <u>number</u> <u>of</u> <u>the</u> <u>dock</u> is three.

10. He is going out the <u>west</u> <u>door</u> <u>of</u> <u>the</u> <u>station</u>.

11. The <u>coat</u> <u>which</u> <u>belongs</u> <u>to</u> <u>the</u> <u>killer</u> is brown.

12. The gunshot hit the house near <u>the</u> <u>head</u> <u>of</u> <u>Sam</u>.

13. They robbed <u>the</u> <u>Jewelry</u> <u>Store</u> <u>which</u> <u>belongs</u> <u>to</u> <u>Jackson</u>.

14. He took <u>the</u> <u>gun</u> <u>which</u> <u>belongs</u> <u>to</u> <u>Pete</u>.

15. He put it on <u>the</u> <u>desk</u> <u>which</u> <u>belongs</u> <u>to</u> <u>Webb</u>.

1. Understanding Life Skills

Savings Accounts

If you have some money, the best place to put it is in the bank. It will be safe. Even if the bank is robbed, you can get your money back. And while your money is in the bank, it will make more money. The bank will pay you *interest.* For example, let's say you put $100 in a bank that pays 5% interest. At the end of a year, the interest will be $5. The bank will pay you $5 in interest. Then you will have $105.

Some banks pay more than others. Before you pick a bank to put your money in, you should find out which bank has the highest interest rate. You can call some of the banks near you and ask what rate of interest they pay on savings accounts. Then you can pick the bank with the highest percent.

To open a regular savings account, first pick the bank you want. Take your money to the counter. Tell the person behind the counter that you want to start a savings account. The teller will give you a card to fill out that looks like the one on the next page.

Signature. The first line says, "Sign here." This means write your name. You must write, not print. Who signed the card in the example?

Social Security Number. On the same line which asks you to sign your name are the letters *S.S. No.* This stands for "social security number." Copy this carefully from your social security card. What is June's social security number?

FRANKLIN SAVINGS BANK

Sign here *June H. Smith*   S.S. No. 756-38-0730

Address **4362 SOUTH STREET**

GLENDALE, NEW YORK 10037

Birthplace **EASTON, NEW YORK**   Date of Birth **7/10/51**

Father's Name **RICHARD**   Mother's Maiden Name **SUSAN**

SMITH   **BROWN**

Name of Husband or Wife _____   Occupation **STORE CLERK**

Date **5/3/79**

Address. The next line asks for your address. Here, and on the rest of the card, you should print, not write. What is June's address?

_____

(Number)   (Street)

_____

(City)   (State)   (Zip Code)

Birthplace and Date of Birth. Next the card asks for your birthplace. Your birthplace is the city and state you were born in. Where was June born?

_____

(City)   (State)

36

On the same line that asks for your birthplace, you are asked your date of birth. This means the month, day and year in which you were born. You can show this in numbers. What is June's date of birth?

These numbers mean that June was born in the 7th month (July). The second number tells the day — July 10. And 51 stands for 1951. So June was born on July 10, 1951.

Father's Name and Mother's Maiden Name. On the next line, you are asked to print your father's name and your mother's maiden name. Her maiden name would be the name she had before she was married. What is the maiden name of June Smith's mother?

Name of Husband or Wife. If you are married, the name of your husband or wife goes on the next line.

Occupation. On the same line, you are asked about your occupation. An occupation is a job. What is June's job?

Date. At the bottom of the card, you fill in the date. This helps the bank know when you opened the savings account. When did June open her account?

After you have filled out the card, you will get a bank book. The bank book will have your account number in it. It will also show how much money you put in the bank to open your account.

Every time you put money in or get it out, you bring the book with you. The bank will mark in it how much money you put in or took out. And, once a month, the bank will add the money you have made that month in interest.

1. Applying Life Skills

Opening a Savings Account

When you open a savings account at a bank, you will be asked to fill out a card like this. As you do the steps below, make sure all the facts are clear. When you are done, change cards with someone in your class to see if everything is right and easy to read.

FRANKLIN SAVINGS BANK

S.S. No.

Sign here _____

Address _____

_____

Birthplace _____

Date of Birth _____

Father's Name _____

Mother's Maiden Name _____

_____   _____

Name of Husband or Wife _____   Occupation _____

Date _____

Step 1 **Sign here.** Write your first name, the first letter of your middle name and your last name. Be careful to write; do not print.

Step 2 **S.S. No.** Write your social security number.

Step 3   Address. Print your street number and name, city, state and zip code. Be careful to print.

Step 4   Birthplace. Print the city and state where you were born.

Step 5   Date of Birth. Using numbers, tell the month, day and year you were born in.

Step 6   Father's Name. Print your father's first and last names.

Step 7   Mother's Maiden Name. Print your mother's first name and last name before she was married.

Step 8   Name of Husband or Wife. If you are married, print your husband's or wife's name.

Step 9   Occupation. Tell what your job is.

Step 10   Date. Use numbers to tell today's date.

2. Preview Words

Study the words in the box. Then read the sentences below with your teacher. Look carefully at the words with lines under them.

another	catch	nearly	robber's
any	frisked	onto	rotor
believe	later	other	second
boss	many	picture	sure
both	might	police	surprised

1. He knew that his <u>boss</u> would be angry at him.
2. It was getting <u>later</u>.
3. He was holding <u>onto</u> the bag.
4. He looked to see how <u>many</u> robbers were in the bank.
5. "You and me <u>both</u>," thought Sam.
6. The man was really looking at the <u>other</u> robber.
7. But then they <u>might</u> die.
8. If I tell them that I can stop time, no one will <u>believe</u> me.
9. He took the gun out of the <u>robber's</u> hand.
10. Sam wanted to make <u>sure</u> that he did not have a gun.
11. Sam <u>nearly</u> jumped back again.
12. Sam <u>frisked</u> the man carefully.
13. He did not find <u>another</u> gun.
14. He ripped the wire off the <u>rotor</u> cap.
15. It is not a get-away car <u>any</u> more.
16. He was <u>surprised</u> when everything started moving again.
17. He stopped just for a <u>second</u>.
18. This gave Sam time to <u>catch</u> up with him.
19. The <u>police</u> came and took the bank robbers away.
20. The people from the newspapers took his <u>picture</u>.

2. The Bank Robbery

Sam was late for work. He knew that his boss would be angry at him. He had been late for work the day before, too.

He nearly wanted to stop time. If he stopped time, he would not be late. The clock would not move. The people on the street would not move. He could walk to work slowly, and he would not be late.

Sam thought about stopping time, but he did not do it. He was afraid. He thought about how the people looked when he stopped time. He thought about how quiet it was. He thought about how he would feel if he had to live like that forever. "I will not stop time unless I have to," he thought.

It was getting later. Sam started to run.

There were lots of people on the street. Some people were going to work, and some people were going shopping. Sam had to run around them.

Suddenly Sam saw a man running out of a bank. The man had a gun, and he had a big bag in his hand. He was running quickly to a car waiting on the street.

Sam did not have time to think. "Time, stop!" he said. Everything stopped. All the people were as still as stone, and everything was quiet.

The bank robber looked as if he were still running. He had one foot up in the air, and he was holding onto the bag. He was pointing his gun at the people in front of him. His face looked angry and afraid. But he was as still as stone, too.

"Now what do I do?" Sam asked himself. He had never seen a bank robber before. He wished that he could ask someone to help him, but he could not. When he stopped time, he was all alone. "It is all up to me," he thought. "It is a good thing that I have lots of time to think."

First he looked to see how many robbers were in the bank. He opened the door of the bank very carefully. He knew that a bird had died when he bumped into it the other day when time was stopped. He did not want anyone to be hurt.

Sam walked into the bank. At first he could not see anyone. Then he saw a line of people in back of the counter, with their backs to the door. Five of them had just turned around when Sam stopped time. They looked as if they were afraid and did not know what to do. "You and me both," thought Sam. He felt better. It did not seem so lonely now.

Sam did not see any robbers in the bank, so he went outside again. He walked past the robber with the gun and looked into the get-away car. The driver of the car was looking right at him! Sam jumped back. The man did not move, and then Sam knew that he was really looking at the other robber. There was a gun on the seat next to him.

"Now what?" Sam asked himself. "What should I do now?" He sat down next to the car to think.

"I could get a rope and tie the robbers up," he said to himself. He thought about how surprised everyone would be. He would get his name in the newspaper, and his girlfriend June would be very happy. He might even get a reward.

"But then I would have to move them," Sam thought, "and they might die. I would not want them to die, even if they are bank robbers. And then everyone would ask me how I did it. What would I tell them? If I tell them that I can stop time, no one will believe me."

Sam looked at the robber who was running to the car. He was still standing with one foot up in the air. Sam knew that he would start to run again when time started again. There was no way to stop him.

"Oh, well, I will have to do it the hard way," Sam said to himself. "It is a good thing that there are a lot of people around to help — when they can move again."

First he went up to the robber who was running to the car. Very carefully, he took the gun out of the robber's hand. He put the gun down on the ground so that it would look as if the robber had dropped it. Then, very carefully, Sam frisked him to make sure that he did not have another gun.

Next, Sam went to the get-away car and opened the door. The driver was still looking right at him, and Sam nearly jumped back again. "What a day!" Sam said to himself.

He took the gun off the seat and put it on the ground near the car. He looked all around in the car for another gun, but he did not find one. "Now I will have to frisk this robber," Sam thought. "I wish that he had looked away when I stopped time." He frisked the man carefully, but he did not find another gun. He got out of the car and closed the door.

Sam had one more thing to do. He opened the hood of the get-away car and ripped the wire off the rotor cap. "When time starts again, this car will not," Sam thought. "It is not a get-away car any more. The robbers will never know what happened to the wire to the rotor cap." Then he closed the hood of the car again.

Now everything was ready. Now Sam could start time again. But he wanted to think. He wanted to be careful that he had thought of everything. He looked at the robber who was running to the car. He walked into the bank and looked around. He looked at the people in back of the counter. He looked at the people who had turned around before time stopped. "I wish that you could help me," Sam thought. "Oh, well, I will get this over with now."

He went outside again. There was the running man, as still as stone. There was the get-away car. It looked the same, but Sam knew that it had stopped. The two guns were on the ground. "Now," Sam said.

He walked up to the running man and got ready. "Time, start!" he said.

Everything started at once—people moving, the sound of cars, everything going at once. Sam had not stopped time for a long time. He was surprised when everything started moving again so suddenly. He nearly stopped to watch everything move. But the robber was getting away!

The robber ran for two or three steps, but then he saw that he had dropped his gun. He stopped, just for a second, but this gave Sam time to catch up with him. Sam jumped on top of him, and they fell to the ground.

At the same time, the driver of the get-away car saw that the motor had stopped. He tried to start it again, but it would not start. He grabbed for his gun on the car seat, but it was not there. He looked for his friend, but someone had jumped on him. He had to get out of there! He jumped out of the car and started to run.

"The other one is getting away!" someone shouted.

"Get him!" Sam shouted. Two men ran after the other robber and jumped on him. They grabbed his arms and dragged him back to the car. Other people came to help Sam with the first robber. "Get his gun!" Sam said. "There it is on the ground." Someone picked up the bag of money. Everyone was shouting and talking at once.

"Did you see that?"

"He just ran up and jumped on him!"

"Wow! The bank was robbed!"

"That man stopped him!"

There were so many people talking at once that Sam nearly felt like stopping everything again. But he was happy. It had worked! He had stopped the bank robbers, and he did not have to tell anyone about stopping time.

The police came and took the bank robbers and their guns. The people from the newspapers came, too. They asked Sam how he did it, and they took his picture. They asked the people in the bank how they felt. Everyone was happy, and everyone wanted to talk to Sam.

Sam had to go with the police to tell them about what had happened. Suddenly he thought, "Oh, no! Now I will *really* be late for work!"

2. Comprehension Questions

Directions. Answer these questions about the story you have just read. Put an *x* in the box beside the best answer to each question.

1. As the story opens, Sam wants to stop time so he can
(B) ☐ a. rob a bank.
   ☐ b. go for a walk.
   ☐ c. be on time for work.
   ☐ d. stay home from work.

2. Sam says to himself, "It is all up to me." This means
(A) that
   ☐ a. stopping a robbery is more than he can handle.
   ☐ b. he does not know what to do.
   ☐ c. he must climb up many stairs.
   ☐ d. he is the only one who can stop the robbery.

3. Sam thought the driver of the get-away car was looking
(D) right at him. Why did this scare Sam?
   ☐ a. He thought the man would find out who he was.
   ☐ b. He forgot that the man could not move.
   ☐ c. He thought he knew the man.
   ☐ d. He was afraid of lots of things.

4. In this story you learn that Sam feels he should not
(E) ☐ a. see June anymore.
   ☐ b. be late for work again.
   ☐ c. be a policeman.
   ☐ d. tell anyone that he can stop time.

5. "What a day!" Sam said to himself. What does this mean?
(A) □ a. Sam was having a crazy day.
    □ b. It had been raining all day.
    □ c. Many good things were happening to Sam.
    □ d. Sam did not know what day it was.

6. Which of these things did Sam do last?
(C) □ a. He frisked the robbers for guns.
    □ b. He stopped time.
    □ c. He made sure the get-away car would not run.
    □ d. He walked into the bank to see how many robbers there were.

7. How did Sam stop the get-away car?
(B) □ a. He ripped the wire off the rotor cap.
    □ b. He let the air out of the tires.
    □ c. He hit the driver over the head.
    □ d. He took out all the gas.

8. What was the last thing Sam did before he started time?
(C) □ a. He checked everything once more.
    □ b. He walked up to the running man and got ready.
    □ c. He pushed the alarm to call the police.
    □ d. He picked up the robber's gun.

9. What kind of person is Sam? He is someone who
(D) □ a. runs away from danger.
    □ b. has big plans but never does anything right.
    □ c. does what has to be done, even if there is danger.
    □ d. feels that stopping a crime is not his job.

10. What is this story mainly about?

(E) ☐ a. How everyone found out that Sam could stop time

☐ b. How Sam stopped some bank robbers

☐ c. How Sam got to be rich

☐ d. How Sam robbed a bank

Skills Used to Answer Questions

A. Recognizing Words in Context   B. Recalling Facts

C. Keeping Events in Order   D. Making Inferences

E. Understanding Main Ideas

2. Language Skills

Plural Possessives

When we want to show that someone owns something, we add 's.

Sam took the <u>robber's</u> gun.

robber + 's

But when two or more people own something, we have to show ownership in another way. Look at this sentence:

The <u>robbers'</u> car would not start.

robbers + '

In this sentence, there are two robbers. They both own the car. The word *robbers* has an *s* on the end to show that we are talking about more than one robber. To make the word *robbers* show ownership, we just add an apostrophe ('): robbers' car.

Exercise 1

Show ownership by adding an apostrophe ('). The first one has been done for you.

1. the <u>hide-out</u> which belongs to the <u>killers</u>

the _____*killers'*_____ _____*hide-out*_____

2. the <u>plan</u> of the <u>robbers</u>

the _____ _____

3. the <u>bags</u> which belong to the <u>shoppers</u>

the _____ _____

4. the <u>bikes</u> which belong to the <u>boys</u>

the _____ _____

5. the <u>mothers</u> of the <u>girls</u>

the _____ _____

Exercise 2

Make the words show ownership by adding the ending to the word. The first two have been done for you.

1. girl + 's   one _____*girl's*_____ coat

2. girls + '   two _____*girls'*_____ coats

3. robber + 's   one _____ gun

4. robbers + '   two _____ guns

5. Mr. Brown + 's   Mr. _____ son

6. Browns + '   the _____ son

7. boy + 's   one _____ pen

8. boys + '   two _____ pens

9. boss + 's   one _____ desk

10. bosses + '   two _____ desks

11. worker + 's   one _____ job

12. workers + '   two _____ jobs

Look at the rules for ownership that we have seen so far.

Rule 1

When the word which shows ownership stands for just *one* person or thing (Sam, boss, car), you add 's.

Sam's house   boss's desk   car's horn

Rule 2

When the word which shows ownership stands for *two or more* people or things, and it ends in s (2 boys, 2 bosses, 3 cars), you add just an '.

boys' bikes   bosses' desks   cars' horns

Now look at this rule:

Rule 3

When the word which shows ownership stands for *two or more* people or things, but it does not end in s (2 men, 2 sheep, 3 policemen), add 's.

men's hats   sheep's tails   policemen's cars

Rule 1 is for words that stand for one: add 's.

Rule 2 is for words that stand for two or more and end in s: add '.

Rule 3 is for words that stand for two or more but do not end is s: add 's.

Exercise 3

Look at the words with lines under them. They show ownership. Tell which rule fits the word. The first one has been done for you.

1. Dan's pen   *Rule 1*

2. many writers' books   _____

3. many men's ties   _____

4. a mailman's truck   _____

5. builders' tools   _____

6. some women's jobs   _____

7. the cook's pans   _____

8. two deer's cages   _____

9. a pile of nurses' caps   _____

10. children's stories   _____

2. Understanding Life Skills

Savings Accounts

When you have a savings account, you can add money to it whenever you like. Putting money in the bank is called "making a deposit." To make a deposit in your savings account, you must fill out a deposit slip. Take a look at the deposit slip shown on page 57.

A deposit slip tells the bank how much money you want to put into your account. It also tells your account number and your name and address. This is so it will be clear which account the money should go into. Let's see how to fill out a deposit slip.

Account Number. Every savings account has its own number. You will find your account number in your bank book. When you make a deposit, you should make sure you write this number carefully on the slip. Then check it. You would not want your money put into someone else's account. What is June's account number?

_____

Date. The deposit slip will have a line for the date. This way, later on, the bank will be able to tell what day you made the deposit on. When did June make her deposit?

_____

Name on Account and Address. In addition to the account number, the bank wants to know the name and address of the person who owns the account. If you are making a

SAVINGS DEPOSIT
FRANKLIN SAVINGS BANK

ACCOUNT NUMBER

089752

DATE _8/5/79_

NAME ON
ACCOUNT _JUNE H. SMITH_

ADDRESS _4362 SOUTH STREET_

GLENDALE, NEW YORK 11227

		DOLLARS	CENTS
CASH		10	90
CHECKS		125	00
		10	00
TOTAL		145	90

deposit to your own account, you would print your own name on the deposit slip. You should spell your name the same way it is spelled on your bank book; do not use a nickname. Be sure to print clearly; do not write. What did June print on the line which asks for "name on account"?

_____

Amount to Be Deposited. The deposit slip shows how much money you will give the bank to deposit in your account. You may have cash (bills and coins) or checks — or both. There is a place on the slip where you write how much you will give them in cash. How much cash did June deposit?

_____

There is also a place on the deposit slip to write how much you will give them in checks. How many checks did June deposit? _____ How much was each check for?

_____   _____

After you have listed the amounts in cash and checks, you add them up and write your answer next to the word "total." What is the total amount that June deposited?

_____

When you have filled out the deposit slip, take it to the counter at the bank. Give the teller the deposit slip, your bank book, and the cash and checks you want to deposit. The teller will mark the deposit in your book and give your book back to you. You should always check your bank book. Make sure the amount marked in your book is the same as the amount of money you gave the teller.

Your deposit will be added to the rest of the money in your account. Then, by looking in the last row of your bank book, you can see how much money you have in your savings account.

2. Applying Life Skills

Filling Out a Deposit Slip

To deposit money in your savings account, you must fill out a deposit slip. Make out the deposit slip on the next page as if you were putting money into your own account by doing the steps below.

Step 1   Account Number. Fill in your account number: 926304.

Step 2   Date. Fill in today's date.

Step 3   Name on Account. Print your name.

Step 4   Address. Print your address: street number and name; city, state and zip code.

Step 5   Cash. Fill in the amount you have in bills and coins: $5.50

Step 6   Checks. Fill in the amounts of two checks: $4.10 and $20.15

Step 7   Total. Add the three amounts and fill in the total.

SAVINGS DEPOSIT

FRANKLIN SAVINGS BANK

ACCOUNT NUMBER

	DOLLARS	CENTS
CASH		
CHECKS		
TOTAL		

DATE _____

NAME ON
ACCOUNT _____

ADDRESS _____

_____

3. Preview Words

Study the words in the box. Then read the sentences below with your teacher. Look carefully at the words with lines under them.

bullets	friends	splash	water
cabin	hero	stake	weren't
couldn't	most	untie	while
didn't	proud	upside-down	windows
don't	scar	wasn't	won't

1. His girlfriend, June, was very <u>proud</u> of him.
2. He <u>didn't</u> see the two men walking in back of him.
3. He tried and tried to move them, but he <u>couldn't</u>.
4. <u>Most</u> of the time he couldn't hear anything.
5. There were no <u>windows</u> and only one door.
6. One had a long <u>scar</u> on his face.
7. No, I <u>don't</u> know why I am here.
8. The man smiled — but it <u>wasn't</u> a friendly smile.
9. You put our <u>friends</u> in jail.
10. "Maybe they will <u>untie</u> me!" Sam thought.
11. Suddenly he felt his hands. They <u>weren't</u> tied!
12. Sam hung <u>upside-down</u> from the stone.
13. He took all the <u>bullets</u> out of the guns.
14. He looked on the deck, and he looked in the <u>cabin</u>.
15. On the deck, he could hear a <u>splash</u>.
16. He <u>won't</u> send any more of our friends to jail.
17. First he jumped into the <u>water</u>.
18. Sam went right to the police <u>while</u> he was still wet.
19. We will <u>stake</u> out the bank.
20. Now you will be a real <u>hero</u>!

3. The Man with the Scar

Life was very good for Sam after he stopped the bank robbers. His picture was in all the newspapers. The bank gave him a reward. His girlfriend, June, was very proud of him. Everyone he knew was proud.

Even Sam's boss was proud of him. He didn't get angry at Sam now if he was late for work. He would just say, "Have you been out jumping on bank robbers again, Sam?"

Sam was very happy. Everything was good.

Then one day it happened. Sam was walking home from work, thinking about going to see June. He didn't see the two men walking in back of him, or the car waiting on the street.

The next thing he knew, he was sitting in a dark room. He was tied to the chair, and his head hurt very much. It was very quiet.

"Where am I?" Sam asked himself. "How did I get here? What happened?" His hands were tied in back of him to the chair. He tried and tried to move them, but he couldn't.

Sam sat in the dark room for a long time. Sometimes he could hear the sound of a car going by. Sometimes he thought that he could hear the sound of waves. Most of the time he couldn't hear anything.

"It feels as if time has stopped," Sam thought. "But even if I stopped time, it wouldn't help. I would still be tied up."

At last a man came in. Then two more men came in. They turned on a light and looked at Sam.

Now Sam could see the room. It was very small. There were no windows and only one door. There was nothing in the room but the chair that Sam was sitting in.

He looked at the three men. They were all big and looked mean. One had a long scar on his face. They all had guns.

"Well, Sam, do you know why you are here?" asked the man with the scar.

"No, I don't know why I am here. What are you going to do to me? How do you know my name?" Sam asked.

The man smiled—but it wasn't a friendly smile. "We saw your name in the newspaper. Now do you know why you are here?"

"No, I don't. I . . ." Then suddenly Sam did know. The bank robbers!

The man with the scar smiled again. "So now you know. You put our friends in jail. Now we are going to get even with you. I bet you were pretty proud that you got your name in the newspaper. Well, now you will wish that you had never had your name in the newspaper. You will wish that you had never met our friends. But it is too late for wishing now."

Two of the men went out of the room. The last man looked at the ropes around Sam's hands. Then he turned out the light and went out. Sam was in the dark again.

Sam tried and tried to move his hands, but he couldn't. At first he was so scared that he couldn't think. Again and again he thought that he could hear the men coming back. He sat in the dark for a long time. At last he went to sleep.

Suddenly the light came on again. The three men were in the room. They were pointing their guns at Sam. "Oh, no!" Sam thought. "This is it!"

One of the men walked in back of him. "Maybe they will untie me!" Sam thought. "Then I can stop time and get away!"

Suddenly Sam felt the man's gun slam down on his head, and everything was dark again.

Sam woke up very slowly. He could feel himself moving, up and down, up and down. He could hear the sound of a motor. Then he could hear the sound of water, very near to his head. He was on a boat!

He was lying face down on the deck of the boat. His head hurt so much that he couldn't move. Suddenly he felt his hands. They weren't tied!

The three men were standing near him, talking. "First we will get rid of him," one of them said. "Then we will make plans for the next bank job."

They came over to where Sam was lying. They thought that he was still out cold. One man picked up a big stone, and

Sam could feel that it was tied to his foot. He could feel the other two men picking him up. His head hurt so much . . . He couldn't move . . . He didn't really care what happened . . .

"Ready!" shouted the first man. "One!"

Sam began to wake up a little more. "What is going on?" he asked himself. He could hear the man shout, "Two!" Sam tried to think . . .

"Three!" shouted the man. The men threw Sam and the stone over the side of the boat.

"Time, stop!" Sam shouted.

Everything stopped—everything but Sam.

The big stone stayed up in the air. The men stood in the boat with their arms up in the air. The waves all around the boat were still.

Sam hung upside-down from the stone. His head nearly bumped the waves.

He woke up fast.

Now what was he going to do? He tried to get up to the stone, but he couldn't. His head still hurt very much. Being upside-down didn't help.

Then he began to swing himself from the rope. At last he could grab the side of the boat. He got up on it and rested until he could untie the rope. The stone stayed up in the air over the waves.

Sam sat down on the deck of the boat and rested for a long time.

When his head felt better, Sam got up. He went up to the men and took all their guns. He took all the bullets out of the guns. He threw the bullets over the side of the boat. Then he put the guns back.

Next, Sam looked all over the boat for guns. He looked on the deck, and he looked in the cabin. When he found a gun, he took out all the bullets and threw them over the side of the boat.

Then he hid himself very carefully in the cabin of the boat. At last he was ready. "Time, start!" he said.

He felt the boat begin to move in the waves again. He could hear the motor running. On the deck, he could hear a splash, and then he could hear the men talking.

The men came down into the cabin. Sam was very, very quiet.

"Well, we took care of him," said one of the men.

"*He* won't send any more of our friends to jail," another man said.

"I don't know," said the man with the scar. "I don't think that I saw him go into the water."

"What?" asked the first man.

"Of course you saw him go in," said the other man.

"*I* saw him go in," said the first man.

"I don't know," said the man with the scar. "There is something funny about it. I saw the stone go into the water, but I don't think I saw him go in."

"Oh, no," thought Sam.

"Are you crazy?" asked the first man. "What did he do— walk away? Of course he went into the water. Now we should get to work."

"Yes, we should get to work," the other man said. "OK, OK," said the man with the scar.

The men sat down to plan the next bank robbery. They went over all the plans. Sam could hear everything they said.

"Now I know all the plans for the robbery!" Sam thought to himself. "But how can I stop the robbery? I will have to tell the police. How can I get them to believe me?"

At last the boat got back to land. The men turned off the motor, tied up the boat, and went up on the dock. Sam stayed in the cabin for a long time, until he knew that they weren't coming back. Then he climbed up out of the cabin.

The boat was tied up right beside the dock. Was it ever good to see land again! But Sam didn't go up on the dock right away. First he jumped into the water. Then he climbed up on the dock and walked into the city.

Sam went right to the police while he was still wet. He told them how the robbers had jumped him and hit him over the head. He told them how he had waked up on the boat, and how the robbers threw him into the water. But he didn't tell them that he had stopped time. He told them that the stone had come untied, so that he could swim to land.

"Before the robbers threw me into the water, while they thought that I was still out cold," Sam told the police, "they talked about the plans for their next bank robbery. I could hear everything." Sam told the police everything the robbers had said.

"We will stake out the bank and wait for the robbers," the police said. "Then we will have all of the gang in jail. You have stopped the gang. Now you will be a real hero!"

"No!" said Sam. "I don't want to be a hero. I don't want to have my picture in the newspapers again."

"Why not?" asked the police.

"The robbers think that I am dead," Sam said. "That is the way I want it. That is the way I want it even when they are in jail."

The next day Sam was reading the newspaper. "**BANK ROBBERY STOPPED!**" it said. "**MOST OF GANG NOW IN JAIL! ONE MAN GETS AWAY!**" Sam looked at the four pictures. There was a picture of the bank robber Sam had jumped on. There was a picture of the driver of the get-away car. There were pictures of two of the men on the boat.

But there was no picture of the man with the scar.

3. Comprehension Questions

Directions. Answer these questions about the story you have just read. Put an *x* in the box beside the best answer to each question.

1. What is the first part of the story mainly about?
(E) ☐ a. Life was very good for Sam.
   ☐ b. Sam stopped a bank robbery.
   ☐ c. Sam's boss was proud of him.
   ☐ d. Sam was thinking about being a policeman.

2. When the men saw Sam on the street, they got him into
(D) their car by
   ☐ a. hitting him over the head.
   ☐ b. pulling a gun on him.
   ☐ c. giving him some money.
   ☐ d. asking him what time it was.

3. Why couldn't Sam get out of the dark room by stopping
(B) time?
   ☐ a. The men were watching him.
   ☐ b. He didn't think he could stop time any more.
   ☐ c. He was still out cold.
   ☐ d. He would still be tied up.

4. Why did the three men want to kill Sam?
(B) ☐ a. He had robbed their car.
   ☐ b. He had put their friends in jail.
   ☐ c. He was trying to kill them.
   ☐ d. He knew too much about them.

5. The man with the scar said to Sam, "Now we are going to
(A) get even with you." This means that they were going to
   - ☐ a. stand next to Sam.
   - ☐ b. hurt Sam for hurting them.
   - ☐ c. take back the money they gave Sam.
   - ☐ d. be fair with Sam.

6. One of the men said, "First we will get rid of him." This
(A) means
   - ☐ a. kill him.
   - ☐ b. hurt him.
   - ☐ c. hide him.
   - ☐ d. tie him up.

7. As the men are about to throw Sam into the water, the
(D) story keeps telling how much Sam's head hurt. This is to
   - ☐ a. give the robbers time to get away.
   - ☐ b. make you afraid that Sam won't wake up in time.
   - ☐ c. make you feel sorry for Sam.
   - ☐ d. let you know how mean the robbers were to Sam.

8. While he was on the boat, Sam could hear the men
(C) planning
   - ☐ a. to get back at him.
   - ☐ b. to kill him.
   - ☐ c. to get their friends out of jail.
   - ☐ d. to rob a bank.

9. What did Sam do the day after the men tried to kill him?

(C) ☐ a. He tried to find out about the gang's plans to rob a bank.

☐ b. He told the police that the gang was going to rob a bank.

☐ c. He read about what happened at the bank in the newspaper.

☐ d. He went to look for the man with the scar.

10. What main thought does the story end with?

(E) ☐ a. The man with the scar would not let anyone take his picture.

☐ b. The police did not believe that the man with the scar was part of the gang.

☐ c. The man with the scar may try to hurt Sam again.

☐ d. Sam wished he had let the newspapers have his picture.

Skills Used to Answer Questions

A. Recognizing Words in Context   B. Recalling Facts

C. Keeping Events in Order   D. Making Inferences

E. Understanding Main Ideas

---

3. Language Skills

The *Not* Contractions

A contraction is a short way of saying two words. Look at these words:

was not ———————⟶ was not ———————⟶ wasn't

did not ———————⟶ did not ———————⟶ didn't

There are many kinds of contractions. We will look only at contractions made with the word *not*.

When we are talking, it is easier to say *wasn't* than to say *was not*. When we make *was not* into one word, the *not* is said so quickly that it seems as if part of it has been left out.

When we write the contraction for *was not,* we do three things:

1. was not   Take out the *o* in *not.*
2. was n't   Put an apostrophe (') to show where the *o* was.
3. wasn't   Take out the space between *was* and *not* to make the two short words into one.

Do these steps to show how *did not* can be written as a contraction:

	did	not
1. Take out the *o* in *not.*	_____	_____
2. Put an apostrophe (') to show where the *o* was.	_____	_____
3. Write the contraction for *did not.*	_____	

Two *not* contractions aren't spelled the same as the others:

will not = won't   can not = can't

Exercise 1

Write the contractions. The first one has been done.

1. had not   *hadn't*

2. can not

3. does not

4. were not

5. has not

6. could not

7. is not

8. do not

9. have not

10. was not

11. will not

12. are not

13. should not

14. would not

15. did not

Exercise 2

As you copy the sentences, write the contractions for the words with lines under them. Then put a line under each contraction. Look at the example in the box before you begin.

Sam <u>did</u> <u>not</u> know where he was.

Sam didn't know where he was.

1. His boss <u>did</u> <u>not</u> get angry.
2. He <u>does</u> <u>not</u> mind if Sam is late.
3. He <u>could</u> <u>not</u> move.
4. Sam <u>did</u> <u>not</u> hear anything.
5. Time <u>had</u> <u>not</u> stopped.
6. Stopping time <u>would</u> <u>not</u> help.
7. No, I <u>do</u> <u>not</u> know why I am here.
8. It <u>was</u> <u>not</u> a friendly smile.
9. His hands <u>were</u> <u>not</u> tied.
10. Sam <u>is</u> <u>not</u> awake yet.
11. Sam <u>has</u> <u>not</u> fallen into the water yet.
12. He <u>can</u> <u>not</u> hurt us now.
13. He <u>will</u> <u>not</u> hurt our friends again.
14. He <u>does</u> <u>not</u> think Sam hit the water.
15. Sam <u>should</u> <u>not</u> let them take his picture.
16. He <u>will</u> <u>not</u> know that Sam is not dead.
17. His picture <u>is</u> <u>not</u> in the newspaper.
18. The police <u>have</u> <u>not</u> found the man with the scar.
19. The police <u>can</u> <u>not</u> find him.
20. We <u>are</u> <u>not</u> going to let her go.

3. Understanding Life Skills

Savings Accounts

There are many uses for a savings account. If you get paid weekly, you may want to deposit money each week. Then at the end of each month, you could withdraw (take out) enough to pay your monthly bills.

You could use the account to save for a trip or a new car. In this case you would keep making deposits and then make one big withdrawal when you have saved enough money. Or you may just save for a rainy day. Then you would withdraw money only for bills you did not know you would have.

No matter how you use savings accounts, you will have to know how to take money out. *Making a withdrawal* means "taking money out." A withdrawal is made by filling out and signing a withdrawal slip. Look at the withdrawal slip on page 77.

Date. There is a place on a withdrawal slip to write the date that you are making the withdrawal. When did June withdraw money from her account?

_____

Account Number. You must also put your account number on the withdrawal slip. If you have more than one savings account, the number will tell the bank which account you want to take money out of. You should copy your account number from your bank book carefully. What account did June withdraw from?

_____

RECEIVED FROM
FRANKLIN SAVINGS BANK   DATE _AUGUST 18, 1979_

One hundred ten _____ $\frac{50}{100}$ **DOLLARS**
(IN WORDS)

ACCOUNT NUMBER   AMOUNT WITHDRAWN

| 089752 | $ | 110 | 50 |

FROM ACCOUNT OF _JUNE H. SMITH_

SIGNATURE _June H. Smith_

ADDRESS _4362 SOUTH STREET_

GLENDALE, NEW YORK 11227

☑ CASH

☐ CHECK

From Account Of. Next you would print your name on the line which says "from account of." The bank will check to see if the name matches the account number you wrote. Be sure to print clearly; do not write. Always print your name as it is in the bank book; do not use a nickname. When June prints her name, she always uses the first letter of her middle name. What is it? _____

Signature. After you have printed your name, you are asked to sign your name. A signature is always written, not printed. The bank needs your signature before it can take money out of your account.

Address. There is also a place on the withdrawal slip for your address. This should be printed so it will be clear. Print June's address on the lines below.

_____

    (Number)   (Street)

_____

(City)   (State)   (Zip Code)

Cash or Check. Your account number, your name and your address all help the bank to know just whose account to take the money out of. Next the bank needs to know how you want the money. They can give you cash or a check. You must tell them which you want by marking it on the slip. Did June ask for cash or a check?

☐ CASH

☐ CHECK

Amount in Numbers. A withdrawal slip has two places for you to write how much you want to withdraw. This is so there will be no mistake about the amount of money that will be taken from your account. The amount is written once in numbers. Copy the amount in numbers from June's withdrawal slip.

AMOUNT WITHDRAWN

$	

When you write an amount in numbers on a withdrawal slip, you put the dollars (110) in the box on the left. You put the cents (50) in the box on the right. You do not write the decimal point (.) at all.

Amount in Words and Numbers. The second time that you write the amount on the withdrawal slip, you must write it in words and numbers. Copy the amount in words and numbers from June's withdrawal slip just the way she wrote it.

_____ $\overline{100}$ DOLLARS
(IN WORDS)

Only the dollars (One hundred ten) are written in words. When you write the dollar amount in words, always begin the first word (One) with a big letter. Always put the first word at the start of the line. Always draw a line after the last word (ten) to use up the rest of the space.

The cents (50) are always written in numbers over 100. Always fill in the space over the 100. If there are no cents, write it like this: $\frac{00}{100}$. Do not use a decimal point (.) this time either.

When you have filled out the withdrawal slip, check the account number and the amounts. Then take it to the counter at the bank. Give the teller the withdrawal slip and your bank book. The teller will mark the withdrawal in your bank book and give it back to you. Always check the amount that was withdrawn from your book to make sure it is right.

Then the teller will give you your money. Be sure to count it carefully *before* you leave the counter. Make sure that the amount of money the teller gives you is the same as the amount that was subtracted from your bank book.

3. Applying Life Skills

Filling Out a Withdrawal Slip

When you want to withdraw money from your savings account, you must fill out a withdrawal slip. Make out the withdrawal slip on the next page as if you were taking money out of your own account by doing the steps below.

Step 1   **Date.** Print today's date.

Step 2   **Account Number.** Fill in your account number: 926304.

Step 3   **From Account of.** Print your name.

Step 4   **Signature.** Write your name.

Step 5   **Address.** Print your address: street number and name; city, state and zip code.

Step 6   **Cash or Check.** Show that you want the money in the form of cash.

Step 7   **Amount in Numbers.** Use numbers to show the amount that you want to withdraw: $105.75

Step 8   **Amount in Words and Numbers.** Write the dollar amount in words (One hundred five ———————). Write the cents in numbers over $\overline{100}$.

RECEIVED FROM
FRANKLIN SAVINGS BANK

DATE _____

(IN WORDS)

ACCOUNT NUMBER _____ $\overline{100}$ DOLLARS

AMOUNT WITHDRAWN

$	

FROM ACCOUNT OF _____

SIGNATURE _____

ADDRESS _____

_____

☐ CASH

☐ CHECK

4. Preview Words

Study the words in the box. Then read the sentences below with your teacher. Look carefully at the words with lines under them.

ago	hopefully	middle	sidewalk
asking	hugging	nodded	those
because	I'll	pale	through
decided	I'm	pointed	unhappy
dreaming	kept	pulled	you're

1. "What about the man with the scar?" he kept <u>asking</u>.
2. Sam <u>kept</u> looking behind him.
3. He <u>decided</u> to tell his girlfriend all about it.
4. <u>I'm</u> going to tell you something.
5. "<u>I'll</u> believe you, Sam," said June.
6. <u>Those</u> bank robbers had some friends.
7. Two days <u>ago</u>, one of them hit me from behind.
8. June turned very <u>pale</u>.
9. You keep saying that <u>you're</u> going to tell me.
10. June looked very <u>unhappy</u>.
11. June looked at Sam <u>hopefully</u>.
12. Sam, do you think you were <u>dreaming</u>?
13. I know <u>because</u> that was how I stopped the robbers.
14. I just think that you have been <u>through</u> a lot.
15. He <u>pointed</u> out the window.
16. June <u>nodded</u> her head.
17. Her head stopped in the <u>middle</u> of a nod.
18. He walked down the <u>sidewalk</u>.
19. Then June <u>pulled</u> him to her.
20. "Yes, I do. I believe you!" she said, <u>hugging</u> him.

4. You Have to Tell Someone

After his little boat trip with the bank robbers, Sam couldn't sleep at night. He couldn't stop thinking. "What about the man with the scar?" he kept asking himself. "He must have some more friends. I could be walking down the street some day, and one of them could get me from behind again. No one would ever know what happened to me. What can I do?"

The next day at work, Sam didn't feel any better. When he walked home after work, he kept looking behind him. "I'm going to go crazy," he said to himself.

At last he decided that he would feel better if he could tell someone all about it. Then someone would know what had happened to him if they got him. He decided to tell his girlfriend all about it. He decided to tell her everything, even about stopping time.

Sam went to June's house the next day after work. "I have to tell you something," he said as soon as he got there. "I'm going to tell you something which will be very hard to believe. But you have to believe me. You just have to."

"I'll believe you, Sam," said June. What is it? Tell me."

"I . . . I don't know how to begin," Sam said. "Well . . . that bank robbery the other day . . ."

"I'm so proud of you, Sam," June broke in.

"Wait! I'm going to tell you about that. But first . . . those bank robbers had some friends. They saw my picture in the newspaper. Two days ago, I was walking home from work, and one of them hit me from behind. They kept me in a dark room for a long time. Then they put me on a boat. They tied a stone to my foot, and they threw me into the water."

"Oh, Sam!" June said. She turned very pale. "Are you all right? What happened? How did you get away?"

STORY 4

85

"I'll tell you how I got away in a little while. First let me tell you what happened. I hid in the cabin of the boat. The robbers didn't know that I was there. I could hear everything they said. They talked about the plans for their next bank robbery. I went to the police and told them all about it. The police stopped the robbery."

"Yes, I read about it in the newspaper," June said. "But I didn't know that you had helped the police."

"I did! You have to believe me. I did help the police. You can ask them. Do you believe me?"

"Of course I believe you," June said. "But how did you get away? Oh, Sam, you could have been killed!"

"I nearly was. Now, June, I'm going to tell you something that will be very hard to believe."

"I'll believe you, Sam."

"Wait until I tell you. Maybe you won't believe me," Sam said. "But I'll tell you. I'll tell you how I stopped the bank robbers, and how I got away from their friends."

"How?" June asked. "You keep saying that you're going to tell me. Tell me!"

Sam stood still and looked at June. Suddenly he wished that he didn't have to tell her. He made himself look at her. He made himself say it. "June, I can stop time."

"What?"

"I can stop time. I can make time stop for everyone but me."

"What are you talking about?" June asked.

"See? I told you that it would be hard to believe," Sam said. "But I *can* stop time. All I have to do is tell time to stop, and it stops. Everyone is as still as stone. No one can move but me. Then I can tell time to start again, and it starts. No one even knows that time has stopped."

June looked very unhappy. "You don't believe me, do you?" Sam asked quietly.

"Well, I . . ." June stopped and looked at him. Then she said hopefully, "Sam, do you think you were dreaming?"

"No, I wasn't dreaming. I know I wasn't dreaming because that was how I stopped the bank robbers."

"It was?"

"Yes," he said. "I was walking down the street, and I saw the robber running out of the bank. I stopped time so that he couldn't move. I took away his gun. Then I went to the get-away car and ripped the wire off the rotor cap so that the car wouldn't start. Then I started time again."

"Oh," June said. She turned away from him and sat down in a chair.

"You see? Everyone thought that I was so brave, but all I did was stop time." June didn't say anything. Sam went on. "That was how I got away when the robbers threw me into the water. Just before I hit the water, I stopped time. Then I hid in the cabin of the boat until we got back to land."

"Oh."

"Is that all you can say? You don't believe me, do you? I told you that you wouldn't believe me." Sam was nearly shouting now.

"But, Sam! I . . . um . . . I just have to think about it. It is all very new to me." June got up and went over to the window. She stood with her back to Sam, looking out the window. "How do you do it?" she asked. "How do you . . . um . . . stop time?"

"I don't know! It just started one day. I just did it." He went over to her and stood beside her. "Do you believe me? Do you?"

"Oh, Sam." She looked up at him, and he saw that she was crying. "I want to believe you. But how can I?"

"Then you think that I'm crazy!"

"No, I don't!" June said. She put her arms around him. "I don't think that you're crazy. I just think that you have been through a lot. First you stopped that bank robbery. You were very brave, but you must have been afraid, too. And now this happens. You're suddenly hit from behind. You're kept in a dark room, and then you're nearly killed. You have been through a lot. You just need a rest."

"No!" Sam shouted. He broke away from her and walked up and down the room. "I'm not crazy! I don't need a rest! I *can* stop time!" June stood by the window. She was crying again.

Suddenly Sam stopped and looked at her. "I'll show you!"

he said. "I don't like to stop time if I don't have to, but I will. I'll do it just to show you."

He pointed out the window. "Look out there. Watch very carefully. I'll stop time, then I'll go out on the street and start time again. Watch very carefully." June nodded her head.

"Time, stop!" Sam said. He looked at June. She looked funny with her head stopped in the middle of a nod. "I hope this works," he thought.

He went out the door and down the steps. It was very quiet. "You don't think about how many sounds you hear all the time," he thought, "until they stop."

He went out into the street. Nothing was moving. He walked down the sidewalk until he could see June's window. There were a lot of people around. "I don't like to do it this way," Sam thought, "but here we go. Time, start!"

A girl on the sidewalk jumped. "Oh! You scared me!" she said. "I didn't see you."

"I'm sorry," Sam said. He looked up at June's window and waved at her. She waved back. Then he walked back up the sidewalk and into the house. June was standing by the door waiting for him.

"Well, what did you think?" he asked her.

"I have never seen anyone get anywhere so quickly!" June said.

"I didn't have to run. I just walked. When I started time again, I scared a girl on the sidewalk. I'll bet she thought that I dropped out of thin air." He looked at June. "Well? Do you believe me? Do you believe that I can stop time?"

"It . . . it is all very new to me, Sam." She put her hand on his arm. "I'll need some time to get used to it." Sam turned away from her. He felt very sad and lonely. They were both quiet. Then June pulled him to her. "Sam, I believe you!" she said.

"You do?"

"Yes, I do. I believe you," she said, hugging him.

Sam felt a little better. He thought to himself, "I don't know if I believe *you*, June. I don't think that you believe me yet. But this will have to do."

Sam smiled at June. "Thank you," he said. "Thank you for telling me that you believe me. Now, there is one more thing."

"What is that?" June asked. She was afraid of what he was going to say next.

"You must not tell anyone about me. You must not tell anyone that I can stop time."

"Oh!" June smiled. "I'll never tell anyone."

"Good," Sam said. He gave June another hug. "I feel better now. I'm not so scared any more. Now if anything happens to me . . ."

"Oh, Sam, be careful!"

"I'll be careful. But if you don't hear from me for a while, tell the police."

"Oh, Sam!"

"I'll be careful! But I'll feel better if I know that the police will look for me. Will you tell them?" Sam asked.

"Yes, but . . . should I . . ."

"Don't tell them that I can stop time."

"OK, but be careful," June said again.

Later, when Sam left June's house, he smiled to himself. "Well, I don't have to be afraid that June will tell anyone that I can stop time," he said to himself. "She won't want anyone to think that her boyfriend is crazy!"

4. Comprehension Questions

Directions. Answer these questions about the story you have just read. Put an *x* in the box beside the best answer to each question.

1. What is this story about?
(E) □ a. Sam hides from the man with the scar.
   □ b. June and Sam have their first fight.
   □ c. Sam tells June that he can stop time.
   □ d. Sam begins to go crazy.

2. Sam was afraid that
(B) □ a. his boss was angry at him.
   □ b. the police were after him.
   □ c. the man with the scar might be after him.
   □ d. June found out that he could stop time.

3. "I'm so proud of you, Sam," June <u>broke in</u>. This means
(A) that June
   □ a. went into someone else's house.
   □ b. started to talk before Sam stopped talking.
   □ c. talked as if she were scared.
   □ d. bumped into Sam.

4. What does Sam tell June about *first*?
(C) □ a. About hearing the plans for the bank robbery
   □ b. About nearly being killed by the gang
   □ c. About being able to stop time
   □ d. About being afraid of the man with the scar

93

5. June says to Sam, "You have been through a lot. You
(D) just need a rest." What is June thinking?
- ☐ a. Sam is just mixed up right now.
- ☐ b. Sam is not telling her the truth.
- ☐ c. Sam really can stop time.
- ☐ d. Sam has gone crazy.

6. When Sam stopped time to show June, he said, "I don't
(D) like to do it this way." Why not?
- ☐ a. He didn't think he should have to show June.
- ☐ b. He would scare people on the street.
- ☐ c. He was tired of stopping time.
- ☐ d. He didn't want to show off.

7. When Sam started time, a girl on the sidewalk <u>jumped</u>.
(A) This means that the girl
- ☐ a. was playing jump rope.
- ☐ b. tried to make Sam fall.
- ☐ c. got hurt when time stopped.
- ☐ d. moved because she was surprised.

8. June says, "Yes, I do. I believe you." What did she do
(C) next?
- ☐ a. She stood by the window.
- ☐ b. She waved at Sam through the window.
- ☐ c. She hugged Sam.
- ☐ d. She nodded her head.

9. Sam told June that if she didn't hear from him she should

(B) □ a. call the police.

□ b. tell his boss that he couldn't go to work.

□ c. look for him.

□ d. call him up.

10. You can tell from this story that June

(E) □ a. cares for Sam very much.

□ b. doesn't know Sam well.

□ c. doesn't really like Sam.

□ d. is afraid of Sam.

Skills Used to Answer Questions	
A. Recognizing Words in Context	B. Recalling Facts
C. Keeping Events in Order	D. Making Inferences
E. Understanding Main Ideas	

4. Language Skills

The *Am, Are, Will* Contractions

A contraction is a short way of saying two words. You know that the contraction *wasn't* is a short way of saying *was not*.

The *Am* Contraction. There is only one *am* contraction:

$$\text{I am} \longrightarrow \text{I am} \longrightarrow \text{I'm}$$

When we write the contraction for *I am,* we do three things:

1. I am   Take out the *a* in *am.*

2. I 'm   Put an apostrophe (') to show where the *a* was.

3. I'm   Write the two short words as one word.

The *Are* Contractions. There are three *are* contractions:

$$\text{we are} \longrightarrow \text{we are} \longrightarrow \text{we're}$$

$$\text{you are} \longrightarrow \text{you are} \longrightarrow \text{you're}$$

$$\text{they are} \longrightarrow \text{they are} \longrightarrow \text{they're}$$

When we write an *are* contraction, we do three things:

1. we are   Take out the *a* in *are.*

2. we 're   Put an apostrophe (') to show where the *a* was.

3. we're   Write the two short words as one word.

Do these steps to show how *you are* can be written as a contraction.

	you	are
1. Take out the *a* in *are*.	_____	_____
2. Put an apostrophe (') to show where the *a* was.	_____	_____
3. Write the contraction for *you are*.	_____	

The *Will* Contractions. Look at these *will* contractions:

I will   ⟶   I͡ wi̶l̶l   ⟶   I'll

you will ⟶ yo͡u wi̶l̶l ⟶ you'll

When you write a *will* contraction, two letters are dropped out, not just one. The apostrophe (') takes the place of *wi*.

Do these steps to show how *he will* can be written as a contraction:

	he	will
1. Take out the *wi* in *will*.	_____	_____
2. Put an apostrophe (') to show where the *wi* was.	_____	_____
3. Write the contraction for *he will*.	_____	

Exercise 1

Write the contractions. The first one has been done for you.

1. you are   *you're*

2. we are   _____

3. they are   _____

4. I am   _____

5. I will   _____

6. you will   _____

7. she will   _____

8. it will   _____

9. we will   _____

10. they will   _____

Exercise 2

As you copy the sentences, write the contractions for the words with lines under them. Then put a line under each contraction. Look at the example in the box before you begin.

I will believe you, Sam.

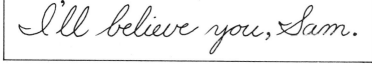

I'll believe you, Sam.

1. She will have to believe me.
2. I am going to tell you something.
3. It will be very hard to believe.
4. You will have to believe me.
5. I will believe you, Sam.
6. You think I am crazy!
7. I don't think that you are crazy.
8. You will be OK after a rest.
9. I will show you.
10. It will take time to get used to it.
11. We will not tell anyone.
12. Tell the police so they will look for me.
13. I'm not afraid that she will tell anyone.
14. They will think her boyfriend is crazy.
15. We will have to be very careful.
16. He will see us.
17. We are near the docks now.
18. He will kill the boy.
19. They are all around us.
20. You are all right now.

4. Understanding Life Skills

Checking Accounts

There are times when you don't want your money in cash. You may want to send some money in the mail. Or you may want to pay a big bill. Then it is best to use a check.

Anyone can have a checking account. You just open an account at a bank. When you open the account, you must deposit (put in) some money. Then the bank will give you a checkbook with blank checks in it. When you want to send money by mail or pay a bill, you can use the money you have put in your checking account. To do this, you just fill out one of your checks and send it to the person you want to pay.

The person can take the check to a bank and get the money. Then the check will be sent to your bank. Your bank will subtract the amount of the check from your checking account. You can add money to your account when it gets low. Then you can write out checks whenever you need to. This is what a check looks like:

KEVIN O'DAY
8 CEDAR ROAD
WILSON, NEW YORK 14172
203
57-33
115

Aug. 6, 19 79

PAY TO THE ORDER OF *Southeast Gas Company* $ *18 62/100*

Eighteen and 62/100 _____ DOLLARS

SAVINGS BANK

Kevin O'Day

⑆ ⑈011500337⑈ 000 605360⑉ 0318

This is a check from Kevin O'Day's checking account. His name and address are printed right on the check. What part of the check shows his name and address? Circle your answer.

Top left   Top right

Each check in your checkbook should be numbered in order. This number is usually printed right on the check in the top right-hand corner. What is the number of Mr. O'Day's check? _____ If the checks are not numbered, you should number them yourself when you get your checkbook.

Here is what you do to fill out a check.

Date. First you write the date on the check. Then you will know when you paid the money to someone. What is the date of check 203?

_____

Pay to the Order Of. Next you write down the name of the person or company that you want to pay the money to. What company is Mr. O'Day paying with check 203?

_____

You must be sure that the name is spelled right and that it is clear. If you don't, the person or company may have trouble cashing the check at the bank and getting the money.

Amount in Numbers. The amount of money that you want the check to be for is written two ways. The first way is in numbers. It is written after the "pay to the order of" line. How much is check 203 for? Copy the amount the way it is written on the check.

$ _____

Check 203 is for $18.62. First you write the dollar amount. Then you write the cents over $\overline{100}$. You do not write the decimal point (.).

Amount in Words and Numbers. The second time you write the amount, you write the dollar amount in words and the cents in numbers. Copy the amount in words and numbers from check 203.

_____ DOLLARS

This is the way $18.62 is written out. The dollar amount is spelled out. Instead of the decimal point, you write "and." The cents are written over $\overline{100}$. Then a line is drawn to use up the rest of the space.

When you write an amount in words and numbers, never use "and" unless it stands for the decimal point (.). Look at this example:

$110.50   RIGHT: One hundred ten and $\frac{50}{100}$

WRONG: One hundred and ten and $\frac{50}{100}$

Signature. The last thing to be done is your signature. On the line at the bottom of the check, you must sign your name. This must be written, not printed. The bank cannot give somebody money from your account without your signature on the check.

4. Applying Life Skills

Writing a Check

Fill out the check on the next page by doing these steps.

Step 1   **Date.** Write today's date.

Step 2   **Pay to the Order Of.** Make your check out to Maria Gomez. Be sure to write the name clearly.

Step 3   **Amount in Numbers.** The amount of the check will be $110.60. Write it in numbers like this:

$$110 \ \frac{60}{100}$$

Step 4   **Amount in Words and Numbers.** Write the amount out like this:

One hundred ten and $\frac{60}{100}$ _____

Step 5   **Signature.** Sign your own name on the line at the bottom. Be sure to write, not print.

501

57-33
115

YOUR OWN NAME
AND ADDRESS
WOULD BE HERE

19 _____

PAY TO THE
ORDER OF _____

$ _____

_____ DOLLARS

_____

SAVINGS BANK

⊕ ⑈011500337⑈ 000 360605⑊ 18 03

5. Preview Words

Study the words in the box. Then read the sentences below with your teacher. Look carefully at the words with lines under them.

ahead	kidnappers'	smashed	that's
already	locker	sped	themselves
driveways	radio	station	unmarked
he's	ransom	stoplight	what's
it's	recorder	streetlamp	wrench

1. The police are waiting for a <u>ransom</u> note.
2. We recorded the call on a tape <u>recorder</u>.
3. We want you to come to the police <u>station</u>.
4. You can tell us if <u>it's</u> the same man.
5. We know that <u>he's</u> a killer.
6. Put the box in <u>locker</u> number 22-A in the train station.
7. <u>That's</u> the man who kidnapped me.
8. They got into the policeman's <u>unmarked</u> car.
9. Cars were <u>already</u> coming the other way.
10. Just then the <u>stoplight</u> turned green.
11. He turned on his <u>radio</u>.
12. The policeman looked in all the <u>driveways</u>.
13. The car was a block <u>ahead</u> of them.
14. We're one block behind the <u>kidnappers'</u> car.
15. The policeman <u>sped</u> up until they had turned the corner.
16. Sam could just see him by the light of a <u>streetlamp</u>.
17. He ran down into the cabin and grabbed a <u>wrench</u>.
18. He <u>smashed</u> as much of it as he could.
19. <u>What's</u> he doing on the boat?
20. The two kidnappers had nearly untied <u>themselves</u>.

5. You!

One day Sam was reading the newspaper. He was looking at the front page. "**BOY KIDNAPPED!**" it said. Sam read all about it.

BOY KIDNAPPED!

Last night Timmy Brown was kidnapped. He is the son of Mr. and Mrs. Ted Brown of State Street. Timmy is six years old.

Timmy was last seen in front of his house. A man saw him getting into a car.

The police are waiting to hear from the kidnappers. They are waiting for a ransom note.

"That's too bad," Sam said to himself. "Mr. and Mrs. Brown must be very sad."

Then Sam turned to the sports page.

The next day, Sam got a call from the police. He was very surprised.

"Did you read about the kidnapping?" the policeman asked him.

"Yes, I did," Sam said.

"Well, we need your help. The boy's mother and father got a call from the kidnapper. He said that the boy's safe. He wants a big ransom."

"But how can I help?" Sam asked.

"We were at the Browns' house when the kidnapper called. We recorded the call on a tape recorder. We think that it's one of the men who kidnapped you. We think that it's the bank robber who got away."

"Oh, no," thought Sam. "Here we go again."

"We want you to come to the police station and hear the tape. You can tell us if it's the same man. If it's the same man, then we must be very careful. We know that he's a killer."

"I know, I know," thought Sam. To the policeman he said, "I'll be right there."

Sam put on his hat and coat and walked down the street. He took a bus downtown and went to the police station.

The policeman put the tape of the kidnapper on the tape recorder. Sam could hear a man saying, "Put $350,000 in small bills in a box. Put the box in locker number 22-A in the train station. Don't call the police or you'll never see your little boy again."

Sam felt cold inside. "That's him," he said. "That's the man who kidnapped me. That's the man with the scar."

The policeman went to his file and took out a picture. Before, Sam had told the police what the man looked like, and they had made the picture then. "Well," said the policeman, "now we know who we're up against. Thank you very much."

Sam put on his hat and coat and started to go. "Wait," said the policeman. "I have to go to the Browns' house now. I'll give you a ride."

They went out of the police station and got into the policeman's unmarked car. As they were driving down the street, Sam was looking out the window at the people on the sidewalk.

Sam saw a man coming out of a store. Suddenly the man turned his head, and Sam could see a scar on his face. "There he is!" Sam shouted to the policeman. "There he is! Stop! It's the man with the scar!"

The policeman pulled over to the side of the street. He and Sam watched the man walk down the street and get into a blue car.

"Maybe he's going to the boy!" Sam said.

"We'll have to be careful or he'll see us," the policeman said. "Don't let him see your face."

Sam pulled his hat down on his head. He could just see under it. The man pulled out into the street and drove past them. Then they pulled out after him.

The man drove down the street and stopped at a red light. Then he turned and drove down a side street. The policeman drove after him.

They drove down the side street. Then the kidnapper's car drove through a yellow light. By the time the policeman got to the stoplight, it was red. Cars were already coming the other way.

"Oh, no!" said Sam. "Now what are we going to do? He's getting away!" He thought about stopping time. But what would he do next?

Just then the stoplight turned green. The policeman stepped on the gas. Soon they could see the blue car at the end of the street.

"He's turning right!" Sam said. When they got to the end of the street, the policeman turned right, too. The blue car was gone.

Quickly the policeman drove down all the nearby streets. He turned on his radio. "Calling all cars. This is car 86. All cars look for a blue 1975 Chevy Nova, plate number YUL615. Do not stop him. Repeat, do not stop him. See where he's going. Report right away if you see him. Over."

The policeman looked in all the driveways and behind all the houses on the street. At last he said, "Well, I think we'll have to give up."

"We're near the docks now," Sam said. "Maybe he's keeping the boy in the same room that they kept me in."

"We should check it out. Do you know where it is?"

"No, I don't. They hit me over the head. I was out cold when they took me there, and they hit me again before they took me away."

"I'll call some other cars, and we'll look in all the houses near the docks," the policeman said. "But first I'll take you home."

As they drove to his house, Sam was thinking. He was thinking about the little boy and the man with the scar. "That man's really bad," Sam thought. "He won't care about the boy. He'll kill the boy if he gets in the way. He might take the ransom and kill the boy anyway."

Sam thought about how scared he had been on the boat.

And this was just a boy. "I have to do something," he said out loud.

The policeman looked over at him. "What?" he asked.

"I want to help. I want to help that boy. Do you think the police will let me?"

"I think so," the policeman said. "I'll call you when something happens."

When Sam got home, he tried to rest. He tried to read the newspaper. He tried to watch TV. But all he could do was to pace up and down in his room. He didn't want to call June because he didn't want to scare her.

All he could do was to wait for the call.

At last the call came. "We're ready to move," the policeman said. "I'll pick you up right away."

"OK, I'm ready."

The policeman and Sam drove by the train station and parked down the street. They couldn't see anyone. "Where are the other policemen?" Sam asked.

"They're all around," the policeman said.

"What do we do now?"

"We wait."

They waited for a long time in the dark. A car drove by. It didn't stop at the train station. They waited. A car stopped at the train station. Sam tried to see the driver of the car in the dark. At last an old man got out and went into the station, and the car drove away. Sam suddenly felt how tightly he was holding onto the car seat. He made himself let go. They waited.

A train pulled into the station. Many people got off the train and came out of the station. Car after car pulled up to pick them up. "He'll come now," Sam thought, "while there are all these people around. How will we know it's him?"

One by one the cars left, until there was no one around. They waited. "This is going to drive me crazy," thought Sam.

They waited.

More cars came. It was time for the next train. People were going in and out of the station.

Suddenly the radio came on. "Calling all cars. A man has made the pick-up. He has on a brown coat and hat. He has the box of money in a blue bag. He's going out the west door of the station now."

"That's us!" said Sam.

They saw the man come out of the station and get into a waiting car. The car pulled out and passed the unmarked police car. The policeman turned on his radio. "This is car 86. He's coming by us in a blue Chevy Nova. We're going after him."

The police car pulled out after the blue car. This time they couldn't let the kidnappers get away. The car was a block ahead of them. Sam looked at the tail lights until he could hardly see.

The policeman turned on the radio again. "This is car 86. We're one block behind the kidnappers' car. We're on Station Street and Green Street. I think we're heading for the docks. Move in. Over."

The kidnappers' car turned left. The policeman sped up until they had turned the corner too, then he dropped back.

Sam was holding onto the car seat so hard that his hands hurt. Yes, that was the blue car ahead of them.

Now they were getting near the docks. What would the kidnappers do? Where was the little boy? Sam's head was spinning with thoughts.

Again the kidnappers' car turned. Again the police car sped up until it turned the corner, then dropped back. Now they were driving by the docks. The policeman turned on the radio to tell the other cars where they were. Suddenly the blue car slowed down, then pulled over to the side of the street. The police car drove past it and quickly turned a corner. "Calling all cars," the policeman said. "The kidnappers have stopped on Dock Street at dock number three. Move in. Over."

Sam could see another police car coming, and then another. The policeman in the unmarked car had pulled over and was getting out. Quickly Sam got out, too. "You be careful," the policeman said. "Don't try to be a hero."

"I won't," Sam said.

Very carefully and quietly, they looked around the corner. Down the street, a man was coming out of a house. He was walking to a boat sitting by the dock with the motor running. Sam could just see him by the light of a streetlamp. He was holding something in his arms.

"It's the boy!" Sam said quietly to the policeman. "He has the boy!"

Suddenly a man came out of the house right next to them. He turned and looked Sam right in the face.

"You!" said the man with the scar.

Then he turned and shouted, "Run! Cops!" Everything happened at once. The other man ran and jumped onto the boat. Policemen ran in from everywhere. Many shots rang out, and a bullet hit the house near Sam's head. The boat pulled away from the dock as more shots rang out.

"Time, stop!" shouted Sam.

It was quiet.

Policemen were everywhere. They looked as if they were running, but they were as still as stone. The boat sat in the still water near the dock.

A bullet hung in the air in front of Sam.

Sam put his hand near the bullet. It was still hot. He ran around the bullet and ran to the dock. The boat had pulled away from the dock, but he could still make it. He jumped over the water and grabbed the side of the boat and pulled himself up onto the deck.

Two men were on the deck, pointing their guns at the policemen. The boy was lying on the deck, all tied up. He looked as if he were dead, but he was still warm.

Sam didn't dare move the boy. He grabbed the men's guns and threw them into the water. He ran down into the cabin and grabbed a wrench. He opened the lid to the motor and smashed as much as he could. He grabbed a rope and ran back up on deck. He ran the rope around one man and then around the other and tied it to the side of the boat. He ran to the boy. He couldn't stand to wait. "Time, start!" he shouted.

The boat rocked, then drifted slowly away from the dock. Sam bent over the boy to see if he was all right. The men on the boat shouted and grabbed at him, but they couldn't reach him.

Policemen came running to the dock from all sides. They were shouting and pointing their guns at Sam and the two men. The policeman from the unmarked car ran up and shouted, "He's OK! That's Sam! He's with me!"

"What do you mean, he's with you?" asked another policeman. "What's he doing on the boat?"

"I don't know," the first policeman said. "But that's Sam, all right."

At last some policemen got into a small boat and came out to the drifting boat. The two kidnappers had nearly untied themselves, but when they saw the policemen, they stopped and held up their hands.

Sam untied the little boy and picked him up. The boy was shaking all over, and he was trying not to cry. Sam held him tight and said over and over, "You're all right now. You're all right now."

The policemen pulled themselves up onto the boat with their guns ready. They still thought that Sam might be a kidnapper. Sam showed them that the boy was all right.

"We should get the motor going and get back to the dock," one of the policemen said.

"We can't," Sam said. "I smashed it with a wrench to stop the boat."

"How did you get on the boat?" the policeman asked.

"I . . . I . . ." Sam began. What was he going to say? He should have gone back to the dock before he started time again! He had never stopped to think! "I jumped. Yes, I jumped on just before the boat left the dock."

"You did? No one saw you!"

"I ran very fast," Sam said.

"Oh," the policeman said. He still had his gun pointed at Sam.

A police boat came and towed the boat back to the dock. The policemen all asked Sam how he had run to the boat so fast. Suddenly Sam thought of something. "The man with the scar! Did you get the man with the scar?" he asked.

"No," said the policeman from the unmarked car. "After he shouted to the other men, we didn't see him again. We have already begun to look in all the houses. He must have a place to hide."

Sam felt sick. Why hadn't he stopped to think? What should he do now? Should he stop time and look for the man all alone? "No," he thought, "if all the policemen can't find him, I never will. Not all alone."

Sam had never felt so lonely.

5. Comprehension Questions

Directions. Answer these questions about the story you have just read. Put an *x* in the box beside the best answer to each question.

1. What is this story about?
(E) ☐ a. Sam gets a job as a policeman.
   ☐ b. The gang robs the Browns.
   ☐ c. A little boy tries to run away from home.
   ☐ d. Sam finds a boy who was kidnapped.

2. Sam read about what happened to the little boy in
(B) ☐ a. a police report.
   ☐ b. the newspaper.
   ☐ c. the note from the kidnappers.
   ☐ d. a note from June.

3. The police called Sam to ask for his help. Sam said to
(A) himself, "Oh, no. <u>Here we go again</u>." What does Sam mean?
   ☐ a. He had just got home from the police station.
   ☐ b. He didn't like getting mixed up with the man with the scar again.
   ☐ c. He was angry that the police kept asking him to help them.
   ☐ d. He knew he would have to ask June to go to the police station.

4. When the police played the tape for Sam, he <u>felt cold</u>
(A) <u>inside</u>. This means that Sam felt
    ☐ a. angry.
    ☐ b. mixed up.
    ☐ c. sick.
    ☐ d. scared.

5. What happened right after Sam told the police that the
(C) man on the tape was the man with the scar?
    ☐ a. Sam read about the kidnapping.
    ☐ b. Sam called the Browns.
    ☐ c. Sam saw the man with the scar.
    ☐ d. Sam and the policeman went to the train station.

6. Sam asked if he could help the police because he
(B)   ☐ a. knew the man with the scar might kill the boy.
    ☐ b. wanted to be a policeman.
    ☐ c. thought he would get a reward.
    ☐ d. wanted to find and kill the man with the scar.

7. What did the man with the scar do right after he saw
(C) Sam?
    ☐ a. He got in a blue car and drove off.
    ☐ b. He picked up the ransom at the train station.
    ☐ c. He ran to the boat.
    ☐ d. He yelled, "Run! Cops!"

8. If Sam had waited any longer to stop time,
(D)   ☐ a. he would have fallen out of the boat.
    ☐ b. the police would have left.
    ☐ c. he would have been killed.
    ☐ d. the man with the scar would have grabbed him.

9. Why didn't Sam stop to think before he started time
(D) again?

    ☐ a. He couldn't wait to see if the boy was all right.

    ☐ b. He wanted to see the look on the kidnappers' faces.

    ☐ c. He was so happy that they had stopped the man with the scar.

    ☐ d. He wanted to show the police that he could stop time.

10. What happened in this story?
(E) ☐ a. The police took the man with the scar away.

    ☐ b. The man with the scar got away again.

    ☐ c. Sam decided never to stop time again.

    ☐ d. Sam told the police that he can stop time.

Skills Used to Answer Questions

A. Recognizing Words in Context	B. Recalling Facts
C. Keeping Events in Order	D. Making Inferences
E. Understanding Main Ideas	

5. Language Skills

The *Is* Contractions

A contraction is a short way of saying two words. You know that *didn't* is a contraction for *did not* and *I'm* is a contraction for *I am*. There are *are* contractions (we're) and *will* (we'll) contractions. There are also contractions made with *is*.

it is   ⟶   it is   ⟶   it's

Sam is   ⟶   Sam is   ⟶   Sam's

When you write an *is* contraction, the *i* in *is* is dropped out, and an apostrophe (') takes its place.

Do these steps to make *he is* a contraction:

	he	is

1. Take out the *i* in *is*.   _____ _____
2. Put an apostrophe (') to show where the *i* was.   _____ _____
3. Write the contraction for *he is*.   _____

Exercise 1

Write the contractions. The first one has been done.

1. he is   *he's*
2. she is   _____
3. it is   _____
4. Sam is   _____
5. June is   _____
6. Webb is   _____
7. what is   _____
8. that is   _____
9. there is   _____
10. where is   _____

Exercise 2

As you copy the sentences, write the contractions for the words with lines under them. Then put a line under each contraction. Look at the example in the box before you begin.

Timmy is six years old.

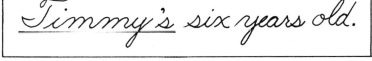

Timmy's six years old.

1. That is too bad.
2. He said that the boy is safe.
3. We think it is the bank robber.
4. We know that he is a killer.
5. Where is he keeping the boy?
6. There is the man with the scar.
7. That man is really bad.
8. He is getting away.
9. What is he doing on the boat?
10. Yes, Sam, it is me.
11. There is one thing we must do first.
12. She is all right.
13. Yes, that is right.
14. What is this?
15. Sam is going to help us.
16. Where is everyone?
17. Hey, the radio is gone!
18. The motor is dead!
19. June is tied up.
20. Everything is fine.

5. Understanding Life Skills

Checking Accounts

When you open a checking account at a bank, you will get a checkbook. Your checkbook will have your checks in it. You can fill out a check whenever you want to pay for something with the money in your checking account.

When you write a check, you must keep a record of it for yourself. Your checkbook will have a part in it that helps you do this. Look at the record kept by Kevin O'Day on the next page.

Check Number. Every check has a number. It is found at the top of the check in the right-hand corner. Look at the record on the next page again. What is the number of the first check that Mr. O'Day wrote?

_____

Date. The date of the check is recorded next. What date did Mr. O'Day write check 101 on?

_____

Payee and Description. After you record the date, you write the name of the person or company that the check is going to. You should write this the very same way you will write it on the check. What company did Mr. O'Day make check 101 out to?

_____

Number	Date	PAYEE AND DESCRIPTION	Amount of Check (−)	Amount of Deposit (+)	Fee (−)	BALANCE
						100 00
101	5/6/79	Central Electric Light Co. electric bill	20 00			−20 00
						80 00
102	5/8/79	Clark's Department Store clothes	30 00			−30 00
						50 00
	5/5/79			100 00		+100 00
						150 00
103	5/20/79	Western Telephone Co. telephone bill	9 50			−9 50
						140 50
104	5/21/79	Mr. Brian Peterson used T.V.	100 00			−100 00
						40 50

On the next line, you write what the payment was for. What was check 101 for?

_____

Amount of Check. In the next row you record the amount of the check. How much was check 101 written for?

_____

Balance. When you write a check, the amount will be taken out of your checking account by the bank. You won't know how much is left in your account unless you keep a record yourself. You do this in your checkbook record. The row which says BALANCE is the part of your record which tells you how much money you have left in your checking account. Look at the row which says BALANCE in Mr. O'Day's record.

How much money did he have in his
account *before* he wrote check 101?   _____

What was the amount of check 101?   _____

How much did he have left in his
account *after* he wrote check 101?   _____

Amount of Deposit. When you add money to your checking account, don't forget to add this to your records also. This way you'll know how much you have in your checking account. First you write the date. Next you write the amount in the row which says "Amount of Deposit." On 5/15/79, how much did Mr. O'Day add to his checking account?

_____

Once you have written the amount in the deposit row, you must also add it to your balance. Look at the row which says BALANCE in Mr. O'Day's record.

How much did he have in the account just *before* he made the deposit on 5/15/79?   _____

How much did he deposit?   +_____

How much was in the account right *after* he made the deposit?   _____

Before you write out a check, take the time to fill out the record in your checkbook as clearly and as fully as you can. This step can keep you from making mistakes, such as writing a check for more than you have in your account. And you will find that a good record of the bills you pay by check is a handy thing to have.

5. Applying Life Skills

Keeping a Checkbook Record

Using the form on the next page, make a record of these checks and deposits. If you need to, look back at the pages which showed how a record should be filled out.

      1. Check number 501
         Written on 6/2/79
         Made out to: Clair Resnick
         For: used lawnmower
         Amount of check: $50.00

Now write $50.00 in the balance row, too, and subtract it from the $200.00.

      2. Deposit made on 6/5/79
         Amount of deposit: $100.00

Now write $100.00 in the balance row, too, and add it to the $150.00.

      3. Check number 502
         Written on 6/10/79
         Made out to: United Insurance Co.
         For: car insurance
         Amount of check: $200.00

Now write $200.00 in the balance row, too, and subtract it from the $250.00.

      4. Deposit made on 6/12/79
         Amount of deposit: $100.00

Now write $100.00 in the balance row, too, and add it to the $50.00.

Number	Date	PAYEE AND DESCRIPTION	Amount of Check (−)	Amount of Deposit (+)	Fee (−)	BALANCE
						200 00

6. Preview Words

Study the words in the box. Then read the sentences below with your teacher. Look carefully at the words with lines under them.

alive	holster	quietly	tonight
becoming	leave	remembered	trigger
bike	let's	risk	unlocked
blindfold	mind	struck	world
done	o'clock	stun	wrote

1. He even thought about <u>becoming</u> a policeman.
2. The man with the scar was going to <u>leave</u> him alone.
3. But when he <u>struck</u>, it wasn't at Sam.
4. He <u>unlocked</u> his door.
5. If you want to see her <u>alive</u>, don't call the police.
6. Come to the corner <u>tonight</u>.
7. At one <u>o'clock</u> Sam couldn't wait any longer.
8. He took out a <u>blindfold</u>.
9. "OK," he said. "<u>Let's</u> go."
10. "What have you <u>done</u> to her?" he shouted.
11. Do you have a <u>stun</u> gun?
12. I can run faster than anyone in the <u>world</u>.
13. He <u>remembered</u> the very first day that he stopped time.
14. He just couldn't take the <u>risk</u>.
15. Then he said very <u>quietly</u>, "Time, stop."
16. He took Pete's gun out of his <u>holster</u>.
17. At last he saw a little boy standing next to a <u>bike</u>.
18. Sam took some paper from the desk and <u>wrote</u> a note.
19. He didn't <u>mind</u> the quiet any more.
20. He stuck his gun out of the window and pulled the <u>trigger</u>.

6. Behind the Brick Wall

Sam was afraid. He was afraid to go to sleep. He was afraid to go out, and he was afraid to stay home. He was afraid all the time that someone was going to get him. He didn't know what to do.

He thought about moving to another house or another city. He even thought about becoming a policeman. But he felt that the man with the scar could find him anywhere.

He spent a lot of time at the police station, helping with reports or just talking. He went to see the little boy who had been kidnapped. He spent a lot of time with his girlfriend, June. He would do anything to keep from being alone.

Days went by. Weeks went by. Little by little, Sam began to feel better. At last he began to think that the man with the scar was going to leave him alone.

Just when he thought that everything was fine, the man with the scar made his move. But when he struck, it wasn't at Sam.

Sam was coming home from work. He unlocked his door, then looked carefully around before going in. "Good," he said to himself. "Another day has gone by, and nothing has happened." Then he saw the note on the table.

"What's this?" he asked himself. "How did it get here?" He opened the note slowly. His hands were shaking. He began to read the note.

Sam:
We know who you are. We know who all your friends are. We watch you everywhere you go.

*We have June. If you want to see her alive,
come to the corner of Brown Street and
Station Street at two o'clock tonight. Don't
call the police. We'll be watching you.*

"June! Oh no, not June!" Sam wanted to scream, to cry, to run to June's house. "Not June! She didn't do anything! Not June!"

He paced quickly up and down the room. He wanted to do something—but there was nothing he could do. There was nothing he could do but wait until it was time to go.

At one o'clock Sam couldn't wait any longer. He picked up the note from June's kidnappers and left the house. He walked down Brown Street until he got to Station Street. There was no one around. He watched a clock in a store on the other side of the street. It seemed as if it weren't moving—it seemed as if time had stopped.

At last the clock said two o'clock. Just then a car pulled up and a door opened. A man said, "Get in, Sam."

Sam got into the back seat of the car. The driver was a man he had never seen before, but the man in the back seat was the man with the scar. The man smiled, but it wasn't a friendly smile. "Yes, Sam, it's me," he said. "I wanted to come for you myself. We'll take you to June now. But first, there's one little thing we must do." He took out a blindfold and tied it tightly around Sam's head. "OK," he said. "Let's go."

They drove for a long time, turning corner after corner. "I don't know where we are," Sam thought, "but I'll bet we haven't gone very far. We're just going around and around."

At last they stopped, and someone opened the door of the car. Sam was pulled out and pushed down some steps. Soon they stopped, and the blindfold was taken off. They were in the same room that Sam had been kept in before they put him on the boat.

Sam turned around and saw June. She was tied to the same chair that he had been tied to. She didn't move.

Sam ran to her and put his arms around her. "What have you done to her?" he shouted.

"Oh, she's all right," said the man with the scar. "We just gave her a little something to make her sleep. She'll wake up soon." He walked out of the room with two of the men. The third man stood by the door.

Sam held June's hand for a long time. At last she woke up. When she saw him, she started to cry. "Oh, Sam," she sobbed, "I just knew that you would come. But what will happen now?"

"I don't know," Sam said. "I don't know."

The men came back into the room. Sam looked at them. "Well, what are you going to do?" he asked. "Now that you have me, will you let her go?"

"We aren't going to let her go just yet," said the man with the scar. "But we might let her go if you give us what we want."

"What do you want?"

"I don't know—but *you* do. You can *do* something. I don't know what it is, but you can do something. You have stopped us three times. How? What do you do? Do you have a stun gun?"

"No, I don't," said Sam. "I don't have a stun gun. I . . . I just run fast."

"*Run* fast?" the man said. "You just run fast? Did you run through the water when we threw you out of the boat?"

"No, I ran into the cabin."

"Into the cabin . . . Then you could hear us. And *you* told the police about the next bank robbery! Why, you . . ."

"Yes, I did," Sam said quickly. "I can run faster than anyone in the world. I can run so fast that people can't see me."

"How do you do it?"

"I don't know. It just started one day. I just do it. I don't know how."

"Well, we'll see about that. We're going to try it out. The Fastest Man in the World is going to help us pull our next robbery."

Sam jumped up. "What?" he cried.

"Yes, that's right." The man with the scar smiled at the other men. "Sam's going to help us on our next job, or Sam's girlfriend isn't going to be around any more." June's eyes were wide with fear. Sam wanted to hit the man with the scar, but the other men were pointing their guns at him.

What could he do? He could stop time, but how would he get June out of there? He remembered the very first day that he stopped time. He had bumped into a little bird, and it fell down. When he had started time again, the bird was dead. Now, every time he stopped time, he was careful not to move anyone too much. So even if he stopped time, he wouldn't dare pick June up and take her away. He just couldn't take the risk.

The man's smile was even bigger. "Yes," he said, "the Fastest Man in the World is stuck now. If he tries to run away, we have his girlfriend. If he tries to call the police, we have his girlfriend. It's just too bad."

"All right, all right, I'll help you," Sam said.

"Good," said the man with the scar. "Who knows? You might like being a robber."

"What do you want me to do?" Sam asked. June was crying now.

"We're going to hit Jackson's Jewelry Store downtown. You're going to run in, grab the jewelry, and run out. Isn't that nice and easy? If you try to call the police, we'll just call Pete on the radio, and you won't see June again. And if you get stopped in the jewelry store . . . you'll be all alone."

"Yes," thought Sam, "just like your other friends who are in jail now."

"OK, let's go," said the man with the scar. He looked at the men behind Sam. "You two come with us. Pete, you stay here and take good care of Sam's girlfriend."

"I will, boss," the third man said.

The first man went out of the room. "Now I'll find out where we are," Sam thought. But just then a blindfold was put on him again.

"We can't have the Fastest Man in the World running back to see his girlfriend, now can we?" said the man with the scar.

Sam waited until he was just walking out of the room. Then he said very quietly, "Time, stop."

Everything stopped.

Sam took off the blindfold and turned around. The man with the scar was right behind him, pointing his gun at him, as still as stone. He had the same mean smile on his face. Sam hung the blindfold over the man's gun.

Sam went back in to June. He wanted to give her a hug, but he was afraid that she might be hurt. He took Pete's gun out of his holster. He took all the bullets out of the gun and put them in his pocket. Then he put the gun back in Pete's holster. He looked at June again. "I'll be back," he said out loud. There was no other sound.

Sam went out of the room. He found himself in a big basement. He turned around and looked at the door of the little room. The back of it had bricks on it. When it was shut, it looked like part of the wall. "That's why the police couldn't find it," Sam thought. Near it was a place for the blue car.

He looked around the basement. He could see the first robber ahead of him, going up some steps. He went past the robber, up the steps, and out onto the street. He was right next to the docks. "I'll bet this is where they kept the little boy, too," Sam thought.

He looked carefully to see which house he had come out of. Then he set out for the police station. He had a long walk ahead of him.

Sam walked and walked. At last he saw a little boy standing next to a bike. He took the bike and said, "I'll bring this right back. You won't even miss it." Then he got on the bike and rode down the street.

When he got to the police station, he walked in and walked past the policemen. They looked as if they were walking around and talking to each other, but they were still. It was very quiet.

Sam was in luck—his friend Webb, the policeman from the unmarked car, was there. He was sitting at a desk. He must have been working on a report when time stopped.

Sam took some paper from the desk and wrote a note.

> *Webb:*
>
> *Please read this note and do what it says right away.*
>
> *The man with the scar and three other men have kidnapped June. They're planning to rob Jackson's Jewelry Store very soon. They're going to make me help them.*
>
> *Get some police cars and stake out the store. Don't move in until I tell you. Then I'll show you where June is.*
>
> *Please don't stop to think about how this note got on your desk. I need you now.*
>
> *Sam*

Sam went out of the police station and got back on the boy's bike. He rode back to the boy and left the bike just the way he had found it. Then he walked back to the house where the bank robbers were. He stood in front of the man with the scar and put on the blindfold.

"Time, start," he said.

"Come on, let's go," said the man with the scar. "We want to be there when the store opens."

They walked out of the room. Sam could hear the big door shut behind them. "Hang on, June," he thought to himself.

The men led Sam through the basement and up the steps. They got into the car again. They turned a lot of corners at first, then drove without turning. When the men took Sam's blindfold off, he saw that they were downtown.

They stopped the car just down the street from Jackson's Jewelry Store. One of the men opened the door. "OK, Sam," said the man with the scar. "You know what to do. But remember that we'll have a gun on you all the time."

Sam got out of the car. He looked up the street. He couldn't see any police cars. Where were they? Why weren't they here yet?

He turned and looked down the street. There was the unmarked car! Webb was sitting in it, looking right at him. The other policemen must be around, too. It felt so good not to be alone any more.

"Come on, Sam," the man with the scar called to him. "Get going."

"OK," Sam said. "Time, stop."

Everything stopped. Sam was getting used to it. He didn't mind the quiet any more. He just got to work.

He opened the hood of the kidnappers' car and ripped the wire off the rotor cap. He took all the bullets out of the men's guns. He took the radio and threw it onto the sidewalk.

He got ready to move. This time the man with the scar wasn't going to get away. "Time, start," he said.

"I said get going!" shouted the man with the scar.

Sam waved at Webb. Suddenly police cars moved in from all sides.

"Hey! Cops!" yelled one of the men.

"What?" shouted the man with the scar. "Pull out! Get Pete on the radio! I'll get Sam!" He stuck his gun out of the window and pulled the trigger. Nothing happened.

"Hey, the radio is gone!" said the first man.

"Let's go! Pull out!" the man with the scar shouted.

"I can't!" said the driver. "The motor's dead!"

"Run!" yelled the first man.

The men jumped out of the car and began to run. But Sam was ready. He jumped on the man with the scar. They landed on the street, and Sam grabbed the man's hands. The policemen ran up and grabbed the other men and frisked them. They pulled the man with the scar to his feet and took him away.

Webb ran up to Sam. "Come on!" Sam said. "I'll show you where June is."

They got into the unmarked car and drove down the street. Three other police cars pulled out behind them.

"OK, tell me," Webb said. "How did you put that note on my desk? How did you stop the kidnappers' car? How do you do it?"

"You won't tell anyone?" Sam asked.

"No, I won't."

"Well . . . I can stop time." Sam told him all about it, from the very first day it happened, right up to stopping the kidnappers' car. "So that's how it all happened. What do you think?" Webb was very quiet. "Do you believe me?"

Webb drove on for a little while without saying anything. Then he smiled at Sam. "Well, Sam, I'll have to think about it. But I do know that you can do something. We need you, Sam. Why don't you become a policeman?"

"I'll have to think about it," Sam said, and he smiled too.

They came to the house by the docks. Sam led the policemen quietly through the basement and showed them the door in the brick wall. They opened the door, ran into the room, and grabbed Pete before he could move. Sam ran to June and untied her.

"Oh, Sam, I knew that you would be back," June said. "I knew that you would save me." She was crying and hugging Sam at the same time.

"We got the man with the scar!" Sam said. "Now everything is all right. Now that the man with the scar is in jail, everything is fine." And he gave June a kiss.

6. Comprehension Questions

Directions. Answer these questions about the story you have just read. Put an *x* in the box beside the best answer to each question.

1. At the start of the story, who is Sam afraid of?
(B) ☐ a. A killer who broke out of jail
☐ b. The man with the scar
☐ c. Someone at work
☐ d. Everyone

2. Just when Sam thought that everything was fine, the man
(A) with the scar <u>made</u> <u>his</u> <u>move</u>. This means he
☐ a. did something to get at Sam.
☐ b. left the city.
☐ c. won a game.
☐ d. decided to live at Sam's house.

3. Why did Sam look around before going into his house?
(D) ☐ a. He didn't want anyone to see him.
☐ b. He was looking for his newspaper.
☐ c. He was looking for a note from the kidnappers.
☐ d. He was afraid someone was waiting for him.

4. What happens in this story?
(E) ☐ a. The man with the scar kidnaps June.
☐ b. Sam becomes a policeman.
☐ c. The man with the scar gets away again.
☐ d. A jewelry store is robbed.

139

5. How did Sam feel when he read the note?
(D) □ a. Too scared to do anything
   □ b. Sad because the gang should have gone after him, not June
   □ c. Sorry for June but glad because he would be safe now
   □ d. Afraid that he would be killed

6. Before they drove Sam to the hide-out, the man with
(C) the scar
   □ a. took Sam to see June.
   □ b. asked Sam what it was he could do.
   □ c. made Sam promise to help him.
   □ d. put a blindfold on Sam.

7. The man with the scar wanted Sam to help them
(B) □ a. rob a bank.
   □ b. rob a jewelry store.
   □ c. get away from the police.
   □ d. get their friends out of jail.

8. The man with the scar said, "We're going to hit Jackson's
(A) Jewelry Store downtown." What did he mean by hit?
   □ a. Burn
   □ b. Smash
   □ c. Rob
   □ d. Bomb

9. When does Sam tell Webb that he can stop time?
(C) ☐ a. While he was spending a lot of time at the police station
☐ b. When he writes the note to Webb
☐ c. When they are at Jackson's Jewelry Store
☐ d. Just before they save June

10. What is the main thing that happens in this story?
(E) ☐ a. A jewelry store is robbed.
☐ b. A little boy is kidnapped.
☐ c. Sam catches the man with the scar.
☐ d. Sam becomes the Fastest Man in the World.

Skills Used to Answer Questions
A. Recognizing Words in Context   B. Recalling Facts
C. Keeping Events in Order   D. Making Inferences
E. Understanding Main Ideas

6. Language Skills

The *Have* and *Would* Contractions

A contraction is a short way of saying two words. There are contractions made with *not* (wasn't), *am* (I'm), *are* (you're), *will* (you'll) and *is* (he's).

The *Have* Contractions. In a *have* contraction, two letters are dropped out, not just one. The apostrophe (') takes the place of *ha*.

I have   ⟶   I ha̮ve   ⟶   I've

Exercise 1

Write the contractions. The first one has been done.

1. they have *they've*   3. we have _____

2. you have _____   4. I have _____

The *Would* Contractions. In a *would* contraction, four letters are dropped out, not just one. The apostrophe (') takes the place of *woul*.

I would   ⟶   I woul̮d   ⟶   I'd

Exercise 2

Write the contractions. The first one has been done.

1. you would *you'd*   4. it would _____

2. he would _____   5. we would _____

3. she would _____   6. they would _____

Exercise 3

As you copy the sentences, write the contractions for the words with lines under them. Then put a line under each contraction. Look at the example in the box before you begin.

He <u>would</u> go to see the little boy.

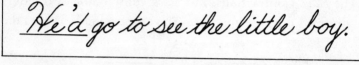
He'd go to see the little boy.

---

1. I wish <u>they would</u> leave me alone.
2. <u>I would</u> be all alone forever.
3. <u>She would</u> like this ring.
4. <u>He would</u> feel better if he told June.
5. <u>I have</u> never seen you before.
6. <u>I would</u> bet we haven't gone far.
7. <u>We have</u> just gone around and around.
8. <u>They have</u> done something to June.
9. I just knew that <u>you would</u> come.
10. <u>You have</u> stopped us three times.
11. <u>It would</u> be better if you'd tell us.
12. <u>They would</u> shoot him.
13. <u>You would</u> be all alone.
14. <u>We would</u> have to hurt June.
15. He was afraid <u>she would</u> be hurt.
16. <u>They have</u> kidnapped June.
17. <u>We have</u> got to stop them.
18. <u>I would</u> just stop time.
19. <u>I have</u> got to think about it.
20. June knew <u>he would</u> save her.

Exercise 4: Review

Write the contractions. The first one has been done for you.

1. would not _____ *wouldn't* _____

2. can not _____

3. I will _____

4. could not _____

5. I would _____

6. what is _____

7. has not _____

8. it will _____

9. is not _____

10. we have _____

11. they will _____

12. she would _____

13. are not _____

14. we will _____

15. they would   _____

16. you are   _____

17. he is   _____

18. did not   _____

19. where is   _____

20. was not   _____

Exercise 5: Review

Tell what words these contractions were made from. The first one has been done for you.

1. doesn't   _____ *does not* _____

2. we're   _____

3. you'll   _____

4. it's   _____

5. I've   _____

6. weren't   _____

7. he'd   _____

8. they're _____

9. I'm _____

10. she's _____

11. you've _____

12. won't _____

13. they've _____

14. she'll _____

15. we'd _____

16. he'll _____

17. aren't _____

18. that's _____

19. there's _____

20. haven't _____

6. Understanding Life Skills

Bank Credit Cards

Banks offer many services. We have looked at two of them: savings accounts and checking accounts. Another service that some banks offer is the *credit card*.

A credit card lets you buy things and pay for them later. Let's say you saw a toaster on sale in a store. It was a good buy, but you didn't have enough money with you. If you had a credit card, you could use it to get the toaster. The store would send the bill to the bank. Then the bank would send a bill to you.

What do you call a card from a bank that lets you buy things and pay for them later?

_____   _____

Two well-known credit cards are "Master Charge" and "VISA." They can be used instead of cash in many places — stores, restaurants and hotels. Every time you buy something with a credit card, the bill is sent to the bank. Once a month the bank adds up the amounts on the bills and tells you how much you owe. The bank does this by sending you a *statement*.

What do you call the paper the bank sends you to let you know how much you have spent with your credit card?

_____

On the statement, the bank lists the names of the places where you've bought something with your credit card. It also lists the amount of each item. The amounts are totaled for you on the statement. This way you know the total amount that you owe. Then you pay the total amount to the bank. The bank pays each place for you.

A credit card can come in handy. If you have a credit card, you don't have to carry lots of cash around with you. Also, if you see something you want but you don't have enough money with you, you can use the credit card to buy it. Then you won't have to make another trip to the store.

But there are things you have to watch out for with a credit card. First, it's easy to spend more than you mean to. It's easy not to think about how much it will all add up to at the end of the month. If you can't pay your bill at the end of the month, then you will have to pay *interest.* This is more money that you will owe the bank. If you can't pay right away, the interest can add up to a lot of money.

The bank will charge you an amount of money for not paying them right away. What is this charge called?

_____

Another thing you have to watch out for is losing your credit card. You must keep your credit card in a safe place. If you lose your card, someone might find it and use it to buy things. You might have to pay for the things they get. So if you lose your card, you must tell the bank right away. Then they will tell the stores to watch out for anyone who tries to use your card.

If you want to get a credit card, you have to fill out a form. You can get the form at the bank. After you fill out the form, you give it to the bank. Then, before giving you a credit card, the bank will check to see if you always pay your bills. If they decide to give you a credit card, they will send it to you in the mail.

Let's see what one of the forms looks like.

NEW YORK NATIONAL BANK
CREDIT CARD APPLICATION

Last Name	First Name	Mid. Initial
JOHNSON	JILL	B.

Social Security No.	Telephone No. (area code)	Number of Dependents
406-29-1401	(212) 226-5402	0

Address   No. & Street   City   State   Zip Code
64 CHASE ST., NEW YORK, NY 10026

How Long		Monthly Payment	Mortgagee or Landlord
3 YRS.	☐ Own ☒ Rent	$200	JAMES WOOD

Previous No. & Street City State Zip Code	How Long
281 PARK DRIVE, LEWIS, NY 12950	5 YRS.

Employer	Position	How Long	Weekly Income
YOUNG FASIONS	DESIGNER	8 YRS.	$210.

Address   No. & Street   City   State   Zip Code
92 SEVENTH AVE., NEW YORK, NY 10001

BANKS & CREDIT REFERENCES

Savings _NEW YORK NATIONAL BANK_

Checking _NEW YORK NATIONAL BANK_

EXXON CREDIT CARD

LANDLORD: JAMES WOOD

OUTSTANDING OBLIGATIONS

REGIS CREDIT UNION $ 500

$

Date	Signature
9/10/79	Jill B. Johnson

Name. The person who filled out this form printed. Who filled out the form?

_____ ____ _____

Social Security Number. Your social security number goes on the next line. Always copy the number carefully from your social security card. What is Jill's social security number?

_____

Telephone Number. There is a space on the form for your phone number. Always fill in your area code and all seven numbers. What is Jill's full phone number?

_____

Number of Dependents. Next the bank wants to know how many people live on your paycheck. A dependent is anyone who does not earn money and must live on the money you make. Your children are your dependents. Does Jill have any dependents? Circle your answer.

Yes   No

Address. Your full address goes on this line. On the next line, you are asked how long you have lived there. How long has Jill lived on Chase Street?

_____

Then you are asked three things: (1) Do you own your own home or do you rent it from someone? (2) How much do you pay a month to live there? And (3) whom do you pay this amount to? Jill rents the place where she lives for $ _____ per month. What is the name of her landlord?

_____

Previous Address. The next line asks where you lived before and for how long. Before Jill moved to Chase Street, where did she live?

_____

How long did she live there?

_____

Employer. This part asks who you work for and where the business is. What company does Jill work for?

_____

What is her job (position) there?

_____

How long has she worked there?

_____

How much does she get paid each week (weekly income)?

_____

Young Fashions is on which New York avenue?

_____

Banks & Credit References. This part of the form helps the bank decide if they should give you a credit card or not. You would write the name(s) of your bank(s) and the names of places they can check to be sure you pay your bills.

At what bank does Jill have her savings and her checking accounts?

_____

Jill has a gasoline credit card with Exxon. She always pays her bill on time. She knows that the Exxon company will tell the bank that she pays her bills. Who else does Jill want the bank to check with to show that she pays her bills?

_____

Outstanding Obligations. This part asks if you owe anybody a lot of money. If you owe a lot of money, then the bank will be afraid you won't be able to pay all your bills. Jill took out a loan at a credit union when she bought her car. How much does she owe?

_____

Does June owe money for anything else? Circle your answer.

Yes   No

Date and Signature. At the bottom of the form you put the date and sign your name. The signature must be written, not printed. When you sign the form, you are telling the bank that everything you have written is true. Always check the form before you sign. Make sure you have not made any mistakes.

6. Applying Life Skills

Applying for a Credit Card

Use the facts below to show how Robert King should fill out the credit card form on page 157. Be sure to **print** clearly. Remember to **write** the signature.

Name . . . . Robert S. King

Social Security Number 092–43–6241
Telephone Number . . . . . (212) 226-6280
Number of Dependents 2

Address . . . . 92 Osborn St.
Easton, NY 10032

How Long . . . . 6 Yrs.
Own/Rent . . . . Rent
Monthly Payment $175
Mortgagee/Landlord . . . . Steven Wicks

Previous Address . . . . . 21 Central St.
Easton, NY 10032
How Long . . . . 2 Yrs.

Employer . . . . Dodd, Inc.
Position . . . . Plumber
How Long . . . . 6 Yrs.
Weekly Income $182

Address . . . . 65 West St.
Easton, NY 10030

Banks & Credit References

Savings	Easton Savings Bank
Checking	Easton National Bank
	Sears credit card
	Landlord: Steven Wicks

Outstanding Obligations . . . None

Date 10/16/79

Signature . . . . Robert S. King

NEW YORK NATIONAL BANK
CREDIT CARD APPLICATION

Last Name	First Name	Mid. Initial

Social Security No.	Telephone No. (area code)	Number of Dependents

Address No. & Street	City	State	Zip Code

How Long	☐ Own ☐ Rent	Monthly Payment	Mortgagee or Landlord

Previous Address No. & Street	City	State	Zip Code	How Long

Employer	Position	How Long	Weekly Income

Address No. & Street	City	State	Zip Code

BANKS & CREDIT REFERENCES

Savings _____

Checking _____

_____

_____

OUTSTANDING OBLIGATIONS

$ _____

$ _____

Date	Signature

TO THE INSTRUCTOR

To the Instructor

Purpose of the Series

Teachers charged with the responsibility of providing instruction for adults and older students with reading difficulties face a major problem: the lack of suitable materials. Stories written at the appropriate level of maturity are too difficult; stories easy enough to read independently are too childish.

The stories in the Adult Learner Series were written to solve the readability problem. The plots and characters in these stories are suitable for adults and older students, yet the stories can be read easily by very low-level readers.

The principal goal of the series is to provide interest and enjoyment for these readers. To this end, every attempt has been made to create a pleasant reading experience and to avoid frustration. The plots move quickly but are kept simple; a few characters are introduced and developed slowly; the same characters are utilized throughout a text; sentence structure and vocabulary are carefully monitored.

A secondary goal is to help adults explore and develop everyday life skills. Lessons and exercises about a variety of life skills provide adults and older students with the basic competencies they need for success in this fast-paced world.

Rounding out the structure of the series are exercises for developing vocabulary skills, comprehension skills, and language skills.

Reading Level

The stories in the Adult Learner Series are all written at second grade reading level. It should be kept in mind, however, that the stories were written for adults: people with a wider range of experience and larger speaking and listening vocabularies than those of elementary school children. Thus, there are some words and some events which might present difficulties for elementary school students but which should not pose problems for older beginning readers.

Besides the slightly increased complexity of vocabulary and plot, the writing style itself has been adapted for older beginning readers. Every effort was made to make the prose sound natural while maintaining simplicity of structure and vocabulary. The repetition of words and phrases has been carefully controlled to permit maximum learning of new words without producing a childish effect.

The reading level of the stories was established by the use of the *Fry Readability Formula* and the *Dale-Chall List of 3,000 Familiar Words.* According to the Fry formula, the range of reading levels in the series is from grade 1.2 to 2.4. Ninety percent of the words used are from the Dale-Chall list.

Structure and Use of the Text

Each book in the Adult Learner Series is divided into several units. Each unit follows a regular format consisting of these sections:

Preview Words. Twenty words from each story are presented for students to preview before reading. The words are listed first in alphabetical order and then shown again in story sequence in sentences relating to the story.

The twenty sentences match the story in readability; students can read the sentences independently. With some classes the instructor may want to read the words and sentences aloud for students to repeat and learn. In very structured classes, the words could also be used for spelling and writing practice.

Story. The primary purpose of the story is to provide interesting material for adult readers. It should be read as a story; the element of pleasure should be present. Because of the second grade reading level, students should be able to read the story on their own.

The pages containing stories are marked throughout the text. Students should be encouraged to return to these pages often and re-read the stories.

Comprehension Questions. Ten multiple-choice comprehension questions follow each story. There are two questions for each of these five comprehension skills:

A. Recognizing Words in Context
B. Recalling Facts
C. Keeping Events in Order
D. Making Inferences
E. Understanding Main Ideas

The letters *A* through *E* appear in the text as labels to identify the questions.

Students should answer the questions immediately after reading the story and correct their answers using the key at the back of the book. Students should circle incorrect responses and check off the correct ones.

The graphs at the back of the book help the instructor keep track of each student's comprehension progress. The *Comprehension Progress Graph* shows comprehension percentage scores. The *Skills Profile Graph* identifies areas of comprehension weakness needing special attention and extra practice.

Language Skills. These sections cover many aspects of language study: phonics, word attack skills, simple grammar, and correct usage. The readability of these sections is higher than that of the stories. The readability level varies depending on the vocabulary load of the specific language skill being taught.

Because the language skills are taught in clear and simple terms, most students will be able to work these sections independently. However, the instructor should be alert for opportunities to explain and further illustrate the content of the lessons.

The lessons contain exercises which give students the opportunity to practice the language skills being taught. An answer key at the back of the book makes it possible for students to correct their work.

Understanding Life Skills. Every story is accompanied by two sections which deal with life skills. The first, "Understanding Life Skills," introduces and fully explains a specific life skill. The life skills all revolve around some detail of modern adult life.

Because this section stresses *understanding* a certain life skill, the reading level is higher than the reading level of the story. However, the life skill lessons are presented in carefully prepared steps, and most students should be able to read and comprehend them without too much difficulty.

Questions used in the lessons are designed to focus the students' attention and to reinforce the learning. Answers for all questions are provided at the back of the book.

Applying Life Skills. Because modern-day living requires both *knowing* and *doing,* two life skills sections follow each story to emphasize both aspects. The second, "Applying Life Skills," is primarily a practical exercise.

This section builds on the understanding generated in the previous section. Students should be able to complete the exercise successfully by applying what they have just read.

Completing this section allows students to demonstrate their mastery of a specific life skill. It gives them the first-hand experience they need with tasks they are likely to encounter in everyday living.

An Answer Key at the back of the book helps students correct their work and gives them immediate feedback.

All units in each book are structured alike, each consisting of the six sections described here. Students quickly discover the regular pattern and are able to work with success and confidence throughout the text.

Summary of the Stories in *The Man Who Stopped Time*

Story 1: The Man Who Stopped Time (Level 1.8) Sam, angry at his girlfriend, June, wishes everything would stop — and it does. He realizes that he can stop time. He steals a pen, then a ring for June, but this makes June angry. Sam threatens to rob a bank, but when he kills a bird by bumping into it, he realizes the dangers in stopping time. He prevents a little girl from being hit by a car.

Story 2: The Bank Robbery (Level 2.2) On his way to work, Sam sees a bank robbery. He stops time, disables the get-away car, and tackles the robbers when time starts again.

Story 3: The Man with the Scar (Level 2.1) The man with the scar kidnaps Sam, holds him in a dark room, then prepares to throw him out of a boat. Sam escapes and reports the plans for the next robbery to the police.

Story 4: You Have to Tell Someone (Level 1.5) Sam tells June that he can stop time. He attempts to prove this to her.

Story 5: You! (Level 2.1) The man with the scar kidnaps a small boy. Sam is called in to help the police. He prevents the kidnappers from escaping with the boy on their boat, but the man with the scar disappears.

Story 6: Behind the Brick Wall (Level 2.2) Sam finds a note telling him that the man with the scar has kidnapped June. He is taken to the hideout, where he is told that to save June he must help rob a jewelry store. He notifies the police, prevents the robbery and the man with the scar is at last captured.

As stated previously, the primary purpose of the stories in *The Man Who Stopped Time* is to provide interesting materials for adult readers and older students. An element of reading for pleasure should always be present.

Readers with second-grade ability should be able to handle the stories with a minimal amount of instructor assistance. Students will need more help with the exercises. The relative ease of these materials should provide a positive experience in reading.

ANSWER KEY

Answer Key
Comprehension Questions

Story 1

1. b	2. a	3. c	4. c	5. d
6. a	7. d	8. b	9. d	10. b

Story 2

1. c	2. d	3. b	4. d	5. a
6. c	7. a	8. b	9. c	10. b

Story 3

1. a	2. a	3. d	4. b	5. b
6. a	7. b	8. d	9. c	10. c

Story 4

1. c	2. c	3. b	4. b	5. a
6. b	7. d	8. c	9. a	10. a

Story 5

1. d	2. b	3. b	4. d	5. c
6. a	7. d	8. c	9. a	10. b

Story 6

1. b	2. a	3. d	4. a	5. b
6. d	7. b	8. c	9. d	10. c

Answer Key
Language Skills

Story 1
Exercise 1

1. the man's car
2. Sam's house
3. the boy's bike
4. June's coat
5. Webb's gun
6. Jackson's store

Exercise 2

1. Sam's girlfriend
2. the girl's eyes
3. the man's smile
4. the boy's father
5. the ring's size
6. the bird's wings
7. the dog's fur
8. the car's horn

Exercise 3

1. The <u>bank's</u> money was in a bag.
2. The <u>car's</u> motor had stopped.
3. Sam was taken to the <u>gang's</u> hide-out.
4. The <u>man's</u> smile was mean.
5. He could hear the <u>boat's</u> motor.
6. Sam went to his <u>girlfriend's</u> house.
7. <u>Timmy's</u> mother was scared.
8. The <u>boy's</u> father got a call.
9. The <u>dock's</u> number is three.
10. He is going out the <u>station's</u> west door.
11. The <u>killer's</u> coat is brown.
12. The gunshot hit the house near <u>Sam's</u> head.
13. They robbed <u>Jackson's</u> Jewelry Store.
14. He took <u>Pete's</u> gun.
15. He put it on <u>Webb's</u> desk.

Story 2

Exercise 1

1. the killers' hide-out
2. the robbers' plan
3. the shoppers' bags
4. the boys' bikes
5. the girls' mothers

Exercise 2

1. girl's	4. robbers'	7. boy's	10. bosses'
2. girls'	5. Brown's	8. boys'	11. worker's
3. robber's	6. Browns'	9. boss's	12. workers'

Exercise 3

1. Rule 1	4. Rule 1	7. Rule 1	10. Rule 3
2. Rule 2	5. Rule 2	8. Rule 3	
3. Rule 3	6. Rule 3	9. Rule 2	

Story 3

Exercise 1

1. hadn't	5. hasn't	9. haven't	13. shouldn't
2. can't	6. couldn't	10. wasn't	14. wouldn't
3. doesn't	7. isn't	11. won't	15. didn't
4. weren't	8. don't	12. aren't	

Exercise 2

1. didn't	6. wouldn't	11. hasn't	16. won't
2. doesn't	7. don't	12. can't	17. isn't
3. couldn't	8. wasn't	13. won't	18. haven't
4. didn't	9. weren't	14. doesn't	19. can't
5. hadn't	10. isn't	15. shouldn't	20. aren't

Story 4
Exercise 1

1. you're	4. I'm	7. she'll	10. they'll
2. we're	5. I'll	8. it'll	
3. they're	6. you'll	9. we'll	

Exercise 2

1. She'll	6. I'm	11. We'll	16. He'll
2. I'm	7. you're	12. they'll	17. We're
3. It'll	8. You'll	13. she'll	18. He'll
4. You'll	9. I'll	14. They'll	19. They're
5. I'll	10. It'll	15. We'll	20. You're

Story 5
Exercise 1

1. he's	4. Sam's	7. what's	10. where's
2. she's	5. June's	8. that's	
3. it's	6. Webb's	9. there's	

Exercise 2

1. That's	6. There's	11. There's	16. Where's
2. boy's	7. man's	12. She's	17. radio's
3. it's	8. He's	13. that's	18. motor's
4. he's	9. What's	14. What's	19. June's
5. Where's	10. it's	15. Sam's	20. Everything's

Story 6

Exercise 1

1. they've
2. you've
3. we've
4. I've

Exercise 2

1. you'd
2. he'd
3. she'd
4. it'd
5. we'd
6. they'd

Exercise 3

1. they'd
2. I'd
3. She'd
4. He'd
5. I've
6. I'd
7. We've
8. They've
9. you'd
10. You've
11. It'd
12. They'd
13. You'd
14. We'd
15. she'd
16. They've
17. We've
18. I'd
19. I've
20. he'd

Exercise 4: Review

1. wouldn't
2. can't
3. I'll
4. couldn't
5. I'd
6. what's
7. hasn't
8. it'll
9. isn't
10. we've
11. they'll
12. she'd
13. aren't
14. we'll
15. they'd
16. you're
17. he's
18. didn't
19. where's
20. wasn't

Exercise 5: Review

1. does not
2. we are
3. you will
4. it is
5. I have
6. were not
7. he would
8. they are
9. I am
10. she is
11. you have
12. will not
13. they have
14. she will
15. we would
16. he will
17. are not
18. that is
19. there is
20. have not

Answer Key
Understanding Life Skills

Story 1

(Signature)   June H. Smith
(Social Security Number)   756-38-0730
(Address)   4362 South Street
                Glendale, New York   10037
(Birthplace)   Easton, New York
(Date of Birth)   7/10/51
(Mother's Maiden Name)   Susan Brown
(Occupation)   Store Clerk
(Date)   5/3/79

Story 2

(Account Number)   089752
(Date)   8/5/79
(Name on Account)   June H. Smith
(Amount to Be Deposited)
   (In cash) $10.90
   (Number of checks)   2
   (Amount of each check) $125.00 $10.00
   (Total amount deposited) $145.90

Story 3
(Date)   August 18, 1979
(Account Number)   089752
(From Account Of)   H.
(Address)   4362 South Street
                Glendale, New York   11227
(Cash or Check)   Cash
(Amount in Numbers) $110.50
(Amount in Words and Numbers)
   One hundred ten ——————— $\frac{50}{100}$

Story 4
Top left
203
(Date) Aug. 6, 1979
(Pay to the Order Of) Southeast Gas Company
(Amount in Numbers) $18 $\frac{62}{100}$
(Amount in Words and Numbers)
   Eighteen and $\frac{62}{100}$ ——————— DOLLARS

Story 5
(Check Number)   101
(Date)   5/6/79
(Payee and Description)   Central Electric Light Co.
                        electric bill
(Amount of Check) $20
(Balance) $100.00
              - 20.00
            $ 80.00
(Amount of Deposit) $100 $ 50.00
                              +100.00
                              $150.00

Story 6

credit card

statement

interest

(Name)   Jill B. Johnson

(Social Security Number)   406—29—1401

(Telephone Number)   (212) 226-5402

(Number of Dependents)   No

(Address)   3 yrs.

$200

James Wood

(Previous Address)   281 Park Drive, Lewis, NY 12950

5 yrs.

(Employer)   Young Fashions

Designer

8 yrs.

$210

Seventh

(Banks & Credit References)   New York National Bank

Landlord: James Wood

(Outstanding Obligations) $500

No

Story 2

SAVINGS DEPOSIT
FRANKLIN SAVINGS BANK

ACCOUNT NUMBER

926304

		DOLLARS	CENTS
CASH		5	50
CHECKS		4	10
		20	15
TOTAL		29	75

DATE [TODAY'S DATE]

NAME ON
ACCOUNT [YOUR NAME]

ADDRESS [YOUR STREET ADDRESS]
[YOUR CITY, STATE ZIP CODE]

Story 3

RECEIVED FROM
FRANKLIN SAVINGS BANK
DATE [TODAY'S DATE]

One hundred five ———————— 75/100 DOLLARS
(IN WORDS)

ACCOUNT NUMBER

926304

AMOUNT WITHDRAWN

$ | 105 | 75

FROM ACCOUNT OF [YOUR NAME]

SIGNATURE [Your Name]

ADDRESS [YOUR STREET ADDRESS]

[YOUR CITY, STATE ZIP CODE]

☑ CASH   ☐ CHECK

Story 4

A check from Maria Gomez:

YOUR OWN NAME
AND ADDRESS
WOULD BE HERE

5 0 1

PAY TO THE
ORDER OF _Maria Gomez_   [TODAY'S DATE] 19____   57-33/115

One hundred ten and 60/100 $ _110 60/100_ _____ DOLLARS

SAVINGS BANK

[Your Name]

⊕ ⑆011500337⑆ 000 360605⑈ 18 03

181

Story 5

Number	Date	PAYEE AND DESCRIPTION	Amount of Check (–)	Amount of Deposit (+)	Fee (–)	BALANCE
						– 200 00
501	6/2/79	Clair Resnick used lawnmower	50 00			–50 / 150 00
	6/5/79			100 00		+100 / 250 00
502	6/10/79	United Insurance Co. car insurance	200 00			–200 00 / 50 00
	6/12/79			100 00		+100 / 150 00

Story 6

NEW YORK NATIONAL BANK
CREDIT CARD APPLICATION

Last Name	First Name	Mid. Initial
KING	ROBERT	S.

Social Security No.	Telephone No. (area code)	Number of Dependents
092-43-6241	(212) 226-6280	2

Address No. & Street	City	State	Zip Code
92 OSBORN ST., EASTON, NY 10032			

How Long	Own / Rent	Monthly Payment	Mortgagee or Landlord
6 YRS.	☐ Own ☒ Rent	$175	STEVEN WICKS

Previous Address No. & Street City State Zip Code	How Long
21 CENTRAL ST., EASTON, NY 10032	2 YRS.

Employer	Position	How Long	Weekly Income
DODD, INC.	PLUMBER	6 YRS.	$182

Address No. & Street	City	State	Zip Code
65 WEST ST., EASTON, NY 10030			

BANKS & CREDIT REFERENCES

Savings ___ EASTON SAVINGS BANK ___

Checking ___ EASTON NATIONAL BANK ___

___ SEARS CREDIT CARD ___

___ LANDLORD: STEVEN WICKS ___

OUTSTANDING OBLIGATIONS

___ NONE ___ $ ___

___ $ ___

Date 10/16/79	Signature Robert S. King

COMPREHENSION PROGRESS GRAPH
AND SKILLS PROFILE GRAPH

How to Use the Comprehension Progress Graph

1. At the top of the graph, find the number of the story you have just read.

2. Follow the line down until it crosses the line for the number of questions you got right.

3. Put a dot • where the lines cross.

4. The numbers on the other side of the graph show your comprehension score.

For example, this graph shows the score of a student who answered 7 questions right for Story 1. The score is 70%.

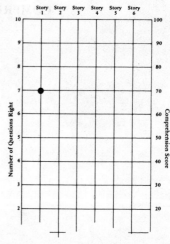

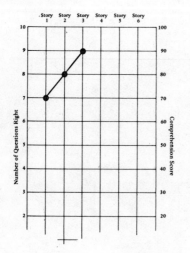

This same student got scores of 80% and 90% on Stories 2 and 3. The line connecting the dots keeps going up. This shows that the student is doing well.

If the line between the dots on your graph does not go up, or if it goes down, see your instructor for help.

Comprehension Progress

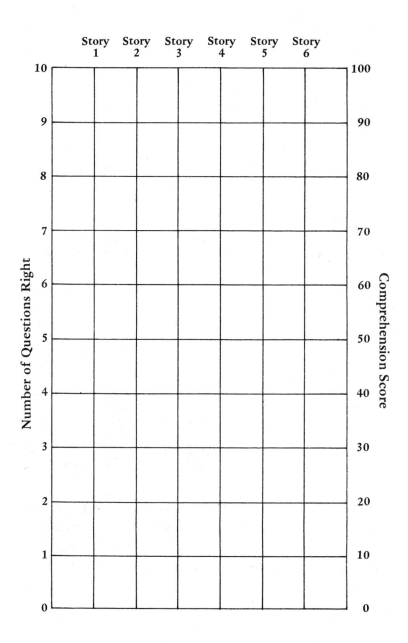

How to Use the Skills Profile Graph

1. There is a block on this graph for every comprehension question in the book.

2. Every time you get a question wrong, fill in a block which has the same letter as the question you got wrong.

For example, if you get an **A** question wrong, fill in a block in the **A** row. Use the right row for each letter.

Look at the graph. It shows the profile of a student who got 3 questions wrong. This student got an **A** question wrong, a **C** question wrong, and a **D** question wrong.

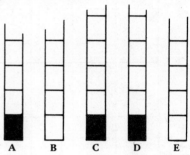

On the next story, this same student got 4 questions wrong and has filled in 4 more blocks.

The graph now looks like this. This student seems to be having trouble on question **C**. This shows a reading skill that needs to be worked on.

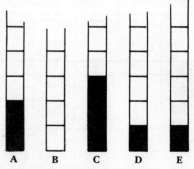

The blocks that are filled in on your graph tell you and your instructor the kinds of questions that give you trouble.

Look for the rows that have the most blocks filled in. These rows will be higher than the others. Talk to your instructor about them. Your instructor may want to give you extra help on these skills.

Skills Profile

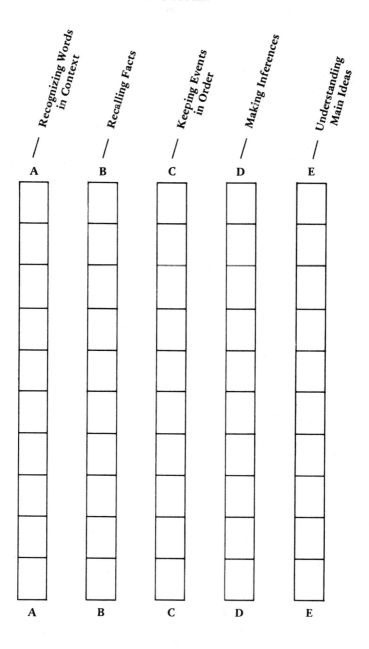

Story	Preview Words	Comprehension Questions	Language Skills	Understanding Life Skills	Applying Life Skills
1. The Man Who Stopped Time	Twenty words from each story are presented for students to preview before reading.	Ten questions with each story feature these skills:	Singular Possessives	Savings Accounts	Opening a Savings Account
2. The Bank Robbery		A. Recognizing Words in Context	Plural Possessives	Savings Accounts	Filling Out a Deposit Slip
3. The Man with the Scar	The words are listed first in alphabetical order and then shown again in story sequence in sentences relating to the story.	B. Recalling Facts C. Keeping Events in Order	The Not Contractions	Savings Accounts	Filling Out a Withdrawal Slip
4. You Have to Tell Someone		D. Making Inferences	The Am, Are, Will Contractions	Checking Accounts	Writing a Check
5. You!		E. Understanding Main Ideas	The Is Contractions	Checking Accounts	Keeping a Checkbook Record
6. Behind the Brick Wall			The Have and Would Contractions	Bank Credit Cards	Applying for a Credit Card